NIXON and ROCKEFELLER

NIXON

&

ROCKEFELLER

a double portrait

STEWART ALSOP

DOUBLEDAY & COMPANY, INC.
GARDEN CITY, NEW YORK
1960

Foreword

It is generally accepted that there ought to be a reason, beyond a wish to eat, for writing a book. The most obvious reason for writing a book about Nelson Aldrich Rockefeller and Richard Milhous Nixon is also the best reason. One or the other might be the next President of the United States. The strengths and weaknesses of the next President of the United States will determine the kind of world our children and our children's children live in—perhaps even whether they have any world to live in at all. The kind of human beings these men are is therefore surely a subject worth writing about.

There is another good reason for writing about them—the simple fact that they are both, each in his own way, quite remarkable and unusual and interesting men. I am not, I

ought perhaps to state at the outset, a hero worshiper of
either man. I admire both Nixon and Rockefeller in some
ways, but I do not admire them in all ways, and I am not
even sure that I shall vote for one or the other of them when
given the opportunity. It is not the purpose of this book to
write a "campaign biography"—rather obviously, since you
can't write a campaign biography of two men who both want
the same job. In fact, it is not the purpose to write biography
of any sort.

I have not tried to tell the whole story of the career of either
Nixon or Rockefeller. I have chosen instead to describe those
episodes in their lives which seem to me to tell something
about them, to help in understanding the sort of men they
are. Understanding them, within the limits imposed by the
mysteries of the human personality, is the purpose of this
book.

Given such a purpose, the book is necessarily in part subjective. It is a portrait of Nixon and Rockefeller, and any
portrait is in the nature of things partly subjective—Stuart's
Washington and Peale's Washington are not easily recognizable as the same man. What seems to me a wen may seem
to another a beauty mark. For example, Nixon's famous rhetorical question—"And incidentally, in mentioning Secretary
Dulles, isn't it wonderful finally to have a Secretary of State
who isn't taken in by the Communists?"—seems to me to sum
up perfectly, in its speciousness and indirection, the case
against Nixon. But I know by experience that to many Nixon
admirers it was a profound and statesmanlike remark. By the
same token, what seems to me to prove an inner toughness of
fiber in Nixon, which would be a major asset in a President,
seems to others to prove that Nixon is unscrupulous or downright evil. Although the contrasts are less sharp, Rockefeller
evokes similarly disparate reactions.

I have done a lot of reporting for this book, ranging from
southern California to northern New England to get my facts,

interviewing scores of people, and taking vast reams of notes. I have tried to report the facts not only accurately but in a reasonably balanced proportion. All the same, this is not what is known as "objective reporting." It is Nixon and Rockefeller as seen through my eyes, and I make no bones about it.

Aside from the fact that each is an interesting man who might be President, there seems to me to be a third reason why it is worth writing a book about Rockefeller and Nixon. As both my brother Joseph Alsop and Walter Lippmann have pointed out, the current vast crop of presidential candidates represents a genuinely new political generation and a sharp break with the past.

There is not a serious Democratic candidate who still parrots the old slogans of the New Deal, as so many Democrats continued to do for a long time after the conditions which had produced the New Deal had wholly changed. Neither Nixon nor Rockefeller evinces the slightest inclination to row back up the river of time, to return somehow to the old days of splendid isolation and low income taxes, as the older generation of Republicans, like Robert A. Taft, longed in their hearts to do. Nixon and Rockefeller, like their Democratic opposite numbers, are men who accept the present, as Margaret Fuller accepted the universe, not because they like it but because there is nothing else to do. Both are ready to go on from here, and both know that it is not only useless but positively dangerous to cast longing glances backward, like Lot's wife.

One thing is certain. Neither a Nixon administration nor a Rockefeller administration would be, even at the outset, a carbon copy of the second Eisenhower administration. Nobody can now safely predict whether history will rate the Eisenhower presidency with a "good," or a "fair," or a "failure." By this writer's lights, the Eisenhower regime has dismally failed to maintain a genuine balance of power with the Communist bloc. But there is another way in which the two

Eisenhower administrations seem to me to have played a good and needful historical role. Despite all the alarms and excursions, the summit conferences, the war scares, and all the rest of it, the Eisenhower years have been a settling-down period, a time of adjustment and stabilization after an era of enormous change—the era of the New Deal, the second world war, and the revolution in American foreign policy of the early Truman years.

A settling-down period was badly needed, if only to help us throw off the neurotic symptoms, like the incredible McCarthy phenomenon, which heavy pressures had generated, and to make us sensible people again. But there are plenty of signs that the settling-down period has gone on quite long enough and may have gone on far too long. The time is coming, and is indeed already here, when the fertility and inventiveness and willingness to experiment of the thirties and forties will be very badly needed if we are to survive the sixties.

Perhaps, in some mysterious way, that need explains the proliferation of able candidates. For it is worth noting not only that there are far more serious presidential candidates this year than in any previous presidential election year— they are also of a very high average level of ability. We need not despair of a political system which, in time of need, can produce a Johnson and a Kennedy, for example, as well as a Nixon and a Rockefeller for the people to choose among.

It is clear, at any rate, that 1960 will be a watershed, a time from which major change will be measured, as 1952 was not. The settling-down period of the last years has been bought with a price, for we have been living on borrowed time. The Republican recapture of the White House in 1952 was supposed to usher in all sorts of radical policy shifts, from a "solution" of the farm problem to "liberation" of the satellites. In fact, the old policies were simply continued at cut rates, under cover of much brouhaha and oratory. After 1960 the old policies will not be continued at cut rates because, in our now drastically altered circumstances, they cannot be.

It is in this context also that it is worth having a good look at Nixon and Rockefeller. They represent the new Republican generation. Because the Republican party is predominantly the conservative party, they also represent the response of the conservative interest in the United States to the challenge of the times. The conservative interest is not monolithic, of course, and the Republican party is a coalition. Nixon and Rockefeller represent the responses to the challenge of what are called, for lack of better words, the conservative and the liberal wings of the party.

There are in fact, it should be noted, no sharp ideological differences between Rockefeller and Nixon, as there were between Dewey and Taft and Eisenhower and Taft. When Rockefeller worked in Washington for the first Eisenhower administration, he often found an ally in Nixon on such issues as foreign aid. The difference is really a difference of style and background and approach to politics—above all, the difference between a professional, partisan politician, a "regular," and a seeming amateur with an air of being above partisanship. It is a choice which has confronted the Republican party before, although in different form.

The choice may already have been made, for all practical purposes, by the time this book is published. That is something the writer cannot foresee. But even if the Rockefeller boom collapses prematurely, Rockefeller will remain an interesting figure, politically and personally. He represents the Republican alternative to Nixon, the likely Republican candidate in 1964 if Nixon wins the nomination and loses the election this year.

For such reasons, at any rate, a book-length look at Nixon and Rockefeller has seemed to me worth the effort to write, and I hope will prove worth the time to read. It is customary in a foreword to acknowledge a debt of gratitude to those who assisted at the literary accouchement. I certainly owe such a debt to that ancient and honorable periodical, the *Saturday Evening Post*.

The editors of the *Post* give a writer all the time he wants to prepare an article, and there is never the faintest suggestion of pressure to conform to any editorial line. They simply give a writer his head, which is why I enjoy writing for the magazine. The only drawback is that a writer occasionally gets carried away with his subject. That happened to me when I wrote an extra-length article about Nixon, and another about Rockefeller, for the *Post*. Squeezing Nixon and Rockefeller into 7,500 words apiece gave me a bad case of indigestion, and this book is designed in part to relieve my literary dyspepsia. Although I have done a lot more reporting for this book since writing the articles, and although the book has been written *de novo*, I have occasionally plagiarized shamelessly from myself. At any rate, if it had not been for Ben Hibbs and Marty Sommers and the other *Post* editors, and their habit of giving a writer his head, this book would doubtless never have been written.

And of course it would never have been written if both Nixon and Rockefeller and dozens of other busy men had not given me a lot of their time. But my greatest debt of gratitude is not to Nixon or Rockefeller or even to the *Post*, but to the American political system itself.

To most Americans, politics is, alas, "not a subject," as the Oxford dons say of an uninteresting topic. Far more people are interested in poker, say, or basketball, than in the unique processes by which the country is governed. Surely this is a pity. For once you have grasped the admittedly peculiar rules of the game, American politics is the greatest of all sports, the most rewarding of all dramas. Where else can you find anything to match the tingling suspense of a convention roll call; or the sudden chance revelation of human grandeur or human squalor at a committee hearing or on the Senate floor;

or the chess-like intellectual challenge of the hunt for a majority coalition of delegates; or the marvelous mixture of complex and compelling personalities, fateful issues, slapstick comedy, great drama, simple silliness, and genuine brilliance which the wonderful spectacle of American politics provides?

The readers of this book are presumably of the elect who have discovered the peculiar fascinations of American politics—otherwise, why read a book about Nixon and Rockefeller? And thus my debt of gratitude to a political system which produces such unusual and interesting men to play the leading roles in its unending drama.

Contents

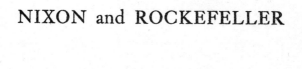

NIXON and ROCKEFELLER

1

Bloviation

A political reporter rarely has a chance to ramble about —to bloviate, to use President Harding's contribution to the language, or, as the British say, to natter. He is hedged in— he must operate within a strict enclosure of a few hundred or a few thousand words. A book is open-ended. A reporter who starts writing a book feels like a horse let out to pasture after too long a time in his confining stall. No doubt that is one reason why journalists like to write books. It is also no doubt a reason why so many books written by journalists are not very good.

Even so, I want to seize this opportunity to bloviate or natter about the nature of the American politician. This may seem an odd way to start a book about Richard Nixon and Nelson Rockefeller. And yet it helps to explain something about them—the fact that they are really a lot more alike in a good many ways than they appear to be on the surface. They share certain well-marked characteristics. And these characteristics, in turn, are shared by almost all major American politicians. Take, for example, the current crop of serious presidential candidates in both parties—Nixon, Rockefeller, Lyndon Johnson, Jack Kennedy, Stuart Symington, Hubert Humphrey, Adlai Stevenson. These seven men are very different in many ways. But with the possible exception of Adlai Stevenson, who is a political sport or mutation, they are also markedly alike in certain other ways.

The first characteristic that all these men share (always bearing in mind that Stevenson is a possible exception) is a Call, or Sense of Mission. They genuinely feel that there is something that they, and only they, can contribute to the nation and the world.[1]

It is extremely fortunate that most important politicians feel this sense of mission, for it is essential to the proper functioning of our political system. Without it, no man who was entirely sane would enter politics, the worst paid and most insecure of professions. Why, after all, should Nelson Rockefeller work harder at the sweaty business of politics than his grandfather worked to become the richest man in the world? Or why should Richard Nixon turn down the firm offer of a law partnership worth over $100,000 a year to run again for Vice-President? Sometimes, of course, the sense of mission is made up largely of a love of power, but there is almost always some element of idealism in it, too. Lyndon Johnson, for example, adores power, revels in power. Yet even the more cyni-

---

[1] *Perhaps the sense of mission explains the odd coincidence that none of the leading candidates smoke cigarettes. Most important politicians feel an obligation to be careful about their health, since their death would be no simple personal tragedy but a national and even global misfortune, or so their sense of mission leads them to believe.*

cal of the Capitol Hill reporters credit him also with a desire to serve his country.

The fact is that the American people, who are politically for the most part a pack of irresponsible boobs, are far better served by their politicians than they deserve to be. Millions of Americans never bother to vote, and most of those who do vote are gold mines of political misinformation, because they are too lazy or indifferent to inform themselves. If they got what they deserved, the American people would be governed by fools and rascals.

And yet look at the U. S. Senate. In that body there are not more than half a dozen fools or rascals. The rest are dedicated to the national interest according to their lights, and among them there are at least twenty men of very superior ability. The American people, who have been taught by those who should know better to regard the word "politician" as a pejorative word, are extremely lucky to have so many good men interesting themselves in the affairs of the nation. And they can thank that call, or sense of mission, or whatever it is that most major politicians have, for their good luck.

Another characteristic of the successful politician is that he is a natural actor of sorts. Almost all politicians have a touch of the ham in them (remember "my little dog, Fala," and his Republican opposite number, Checkers) but they need more than mere hamminess. A major politician must be, like a great actor, hypersensitive to the reactions and emotions of other people. He must be able to "smell the mood of the Senate," as Lyndon Johnson is able to do, or even to smell the mood of a whole nation, as Franklin Roosevelt was often (though not always) able to do. At the same time, a major politician, again like an actor, must be able to affect the mood of his audience, to move people to sympathy or anger or enthusiasm.

There is so much unnatural emphasis nowadays on naturalness, so much insincere guff about sincerity, that most politicians try to pretend that they never pretend. And yet a leading politician cannot possibly be natural—he must rather often appear to be what his audience wants and expects him to be rather than what he is. So a politician builds up by layers a thick carapace, a protective outer shell which he turns to the world. All of us, to be sure, sprout such a carapace in time, but the carapace of a politician is particularly thick.

This is true of all the leading presidential contenders, but it is especially true of Nixon and Rockefeller. Virtually all enormously rich men grow by necessity a thick shell to protect them from the envious and rapacious world, and Rockefeller thus wears both the rich man's and the politician's carapace. As for Nixon, he is by nature strangely reserved and with-drawn for a politician. "I can't really let my hair down with anyone, anyone at all," Nixon once remarked to me, which was his way of saying that he is never without his outer protective shell.

In writing about politicians, I have found that a good way to pierce the carapace, to find out something about what really lies beneath the outer shell, is to search out the boy who was father of the man. It is for that reason that I traveled to Whittier, California, where Nixon was brought up, and to Hanover, New Hampshire, where Rockefeller went to college, to talk to their teachers and to others who remembered them when they were boys. It was for the same reason that I wrote letters of inquiry to Rockefeller's and Nixon's classmates— excerpts from the responses, some of which give a sudden vivid picture of the boys these men used to be, are included in the appendix.

This technique of turning the clock back reveals certain other characteristics which almost all leading politicians share. Almost all important politicians were Big Men On Campus—BMOCs—in their college days. A survey would probably show that at least half the present members of the Senate were presidents of their college classes, or something

of the sort. From the time he was in knickerbockers in high
school until he graduated from Duke University Law School,
Nixon ran for class president or the equivalent with clocklike
regularity. Rockefeller ran for the class presidency at Dartmouth, and he was beaten only by political bad management;
he split the vote of the more powerful fraternities with another man, and a dark horse won.

With the possible exception of Adlai Stevenson (the
chronic exception—Stevenson was not really designed by nature to be a politician), the other presidential aspirants were
without exception BMOCs, despite the fact that none of them
was a first-class athlete. The athletic field is easiest place to
become a BMOC, but a surprising number of successful politicians became BMOCs by their prowess as debaters.

This is not true of those, like Kennedy, Stevenson, and
Rockefeller, who went to Ivy League colleges, where debating is no asset to a man's college career. But west of the
Alleghenies there are many colleges in which the debate team
—often so called—is the non-athlete's substitute for the football team. These debate teams have many distinguished
graduates.

Nixon was the champion debater of southern California,
and I am convinced, as I shall try to show later, that his
experience as a college debater had a lot to do with the sort
of politician Nixon became. Hubert Humphrey was not only
a champion debater—he also became a debating coach and
speech teacher, which may account for the seeming glibness
which is Humphrey's greatest drawback as a presidential
candidate.

The Senate is crawling with former champion debaters—
Smathers of Florida and Mundt of South Dakota, to cite a
couple of examples, were state champions. Lyndon Johnson
was almost champion of Texas. "We won sixty-five or sixty-six
debates," Johnson once told me, "only lost the last one. When
that last judge voted against us, for the state championship,

I was so disappointed I went right into the bathroom and was sick."

The curious mental image which this reminiscence evokes, of the future Majority Leader vomiting in the anguish of his disappointment, suggests another characteristic which almost all successful politicians share—a horror of failure. In some cases this hatred of failure can reach a point where a normally upright and honorable politician will all but sell his soul to avoid defeat. The other side of the coin is an astonishing drive and ambition.

The current crop of presidential aspirants (again with the possible exception of Stevenson, and perhaps Pat Brown of California, if you consider him a serious candidate) have these qualities to a really remarkable degree. They are fiercely, abnormally, one is almost tempted to say pathologically, ambitious. I once asked Lyndon Johnson where he got his extraordinary drive. "Well, I suppose you'd call it pride," he said. "Almost everybody has pride—I suppose you want to do a good job as a writer. But some people have it to an unusual degree."

"Unusual" is far too mild a word. The life of a politician is a grueling one in any case, especially at campaign time. But the politician who aspires to the presidency must have "pride" to such an "unusual degree" that he is prepared to go through the modern equivalent of the ordeal by fire many times over. And although Johnson has this quality of pride, or ambition, or drive, or call it what you will, to an exceedingly unusual degree, there is one man who has it to an even more unusual degree, and that is Richard Nixon. And if there is one man who has it to an even more unusual degree than Nixon, his name—a fact which will surprise those who know him casually as an amiable fellow with a big grin—is Nelson Rockefeller.

Ambition is no bad thing—what man without great ambition has greatly achieved? And yet again, ambition, above all, ambition for the presidency, is something that every politician learns to conceal as best he may, and as long as possible.

Malcolm Muggeridge, former editor of *Punch,* is one of the few Englishmen who have caught something of the fascination of American politics. He invented Muggeridge's Law at the 1952 Republican convention, when Robert A. Taft made his third and last unsuccessful bid for the Republican nomination. Muggeridge recalled what most grown men know—that the boy who wants the girl too much doesn't get her. If he is desperate for her, his eyes bug out, his palms sweat, and his voice sounds like the croak of an expiring raven, so that he appears a ludicrous and wholly unlovable figure to his lady love. Another boy, who really doesn't care very much whether or not she says "yes," will sweep her off her feet. The poet William Blake summed it up rather neatly:

> *I told my love, I told my love,*
> *I told her all my heart,*
> *Trembling, cold, in ghastly fears.*
> *Ah! she did depart!*
>
> *Soon after she was gone from me,*
> *A traveller came by,*
> *Silently, invisibly:*
> *He took her with a sigh.*

Thus Muggeridge's Law reads: "If the candidate wants it too much, the convention turns him down." The law has been proved again and again in recent years—the names of Estes Kefauver, Harold Stassen, and Averell Harriman come to mind, as well as that of Taft, with Eisenhower and Stevenson the most recent examples of the sighing traveler. Nixon is very well aware of Muggeridge's Law, as his comments in the talk preserved in the appendix of this book suggest. So are all the other candidates. Muggeridge's Law creates a special problem for Rockefeller, moreover, since as challenger it is particularly difficult for him to avoid a fatal appearance of overeagerness—which is why Rockefeller might conceivably be out of the running even before this book is published.

Being a presidential candidate, especially an unacknowledged one, must be a hideously difficult way of life, more difficult in some ways than the presidency itself. The candidate ought to be, or appear to be, a friend to all the world, relaxed, happy, outgiving, easy with the handshake, the sincere smile, the clap on the back. He ought to be a "buddy-buddy boy," to use a horrible phrase Nixon once used to me. It was because he was not a buddy-buddy boy that Thomas E. Dewey never became President (and in his failure almost drove the Republican party mad). It was partly because he was not a buddy-buddy boy that Taft failed thrice to get the nomination, and it was partly for the same reason that Adlai Stevenson ran twice so disastrously behind Dwight Eisenhower. And it is because he is not a buddy-buddy boy that Nixon himself, as he is well aware, may yet fail to seize the prize which is almost, as this is written, within his grasp.

But while appearing as a friend to all the world, the ideal candidate must also manage to convey an aura of presidential dignity, a seriousness of mien worthy of the great office he seeks, being careful at the same time not to cross the invisible line which separates dignity from a laughable stuffiness. And all the while he must watch his step as though treading among rattlesnakes, and watch his words as though the wrong one might be his death warrant. Nixon is not alone— no serious aspirant to the presidency can *really* let down his hair with anyone at all.

Above all, a serious candidate for the presidency must be tough, tough as a whole hogshead of nails. He must be physically tough—for he must be ready to carry on with smiling seeming-confidence when he feels like death. And he must be tough in another way, too, with a toughness that never surrenders, even when the smell of defeat is thick and heavy in the air. This toughness is another quality which Nixon and Rockefeller share with all but one of the serious Democratic contenders. It is not surprising, surely, that men who have these special qualities, and who can therefore play the impossible role of presidential candidate, are *sui generis*, a race apart, however much they may differ in appearance, accent, or ideology.

This suggests one reason why our political system, by its peculiar workings, has produced a large number of good Presidents, and several great Presidents. All the qualities which a successful candidate must have are also qualities markedly useful in a President.

2

What Everybody Knows

The one thing almost all Americans know about Nelson Rockefeller is that he is rich. The one thing almost all Americans know about Richard Nixon is whether they like him or dislike him. Both are important things to know about both men.

The fact that Rockefeller is rich has colored his whole life, and it will certainly greatly influence his political future. The fact that Nixon has the capacity, rare among American politicians nowadays, to arouse strong emotions has also colored his whole life, and will also greatly influence his political future. So before going on to examine some of the facts that not everybody knows about these two remarkable men, let us have a look at these two facts that everybody knows about them.

Consider Nixon's idiosyncrasy first. This is the era of the bland, or non-controversial, politician. It is the era when the ancient political art of being all things to all men (and, since the Nineteenth Amendment, all women) has been developed to its logical conclusion. As former Senator George H. Bender, faithful servitor of both capitalist George Humphrey and unionist James Hoffa, has remarked: "You don't have to become a prostitute yourself, but you have to get their votes." Because it is considered necessary to get the votes of prostitutes, and of every other conceivable voting group, from the anti-vivisectionists to the homosexuals,[1] most politicians, most of the time, are conscientiously nice to quite literally everybody. The result is that very few politicians arouse really strong emotions in anybody's breast.

Nixon arouses strong emotions in almost everybody's breast. That is the special mark of the man. Nor is this peculiarity limited to those who know him, or even those personally involved in the political process, as one learns from the instructive experience of going out and ringing doorbells

---

[1] *One story has always amused me, although I can't prove that it is true. In the beginning of the McCarthy era it was revealed that some eighty-odd State Department officials had been fired because of homosexual tendencies. The right-wing Republicans, led by the late Kenneth Wherry of Nebraska, known as the "merry undertaker," seized with delight on this "issue." For a time, the "homosexual issue" bid fair to rival the "Communist issue." But then—or so the story goes—some bright young man in Republican headquarters dipped into a best seller of those days, the Kinsey report on the sexual habits of the American male. A quick calculation based on Kinsey's figures showed that there must be several million American homosexuals of voting age. The bright young man realized that it would be extremely dangerous politically for the Republican party to be considered the anti-homosexual party—almost as dangerous as to be considered the anti-Negro or anti-Polish or anti-Jewish party. He so reported to the Republican leadership. The "homosexual issue" was instantly dropped.*

and talking to large numbers of citizens. Most other important political names are likely to elicit a vague and impersonal
reaction—"I kinda like him," or "I just don't go for him too
much." Not Nixon's. Nixon's name almost always elicits a
clear and explicit response, quite often of real admiration,
quite often of something like hatred. Most people have a
vivid mental image of Nixon, and the image either wears a
halo or has cloven hoofs and a tail.

There are perfectly rational reasons for disliking Nixon,
just as there are perfectly rational reasons for admiring him.
But what is striking about both the Nixonophiles and the
Nixonophobes is the marked irrational content in the attitudes of both. I remember the old lady in Whittier, California, Nixon's home town, who called me up when she heard
I was in town to write about Nixon to say: "I know it's against
religion to hate anybody, but I just can't help hating that
Nixon. He's just like that Hitler." I also remember the rather
embarrassing luncheon with a college classmate and admirer
of Nixon's, whose eyes filled with tears as he kept repeating,
"He's a real wonderful guy."

Nixon arouses such unreasoned and extreme reactions on
more sophisticated levels as well. There are many regular
Republicans, especially in the Midwest, who hate and fear
Nelson Rockefeller simply because he may threaten the presidential chances of "our boy, Dick." Especially among the
more conservative Republicans, the admirers of the late
Robert A. Taft, any criticism of Nixon is likely to be equated
with subversion. The admiration for Nixon among the Taft-
worshipers is essentially irrational, since Nixon contributed
to Taft's last defeat in 1952 and since he has none of Taft's
hankering for a simpler past. But the admiration for Nixon
among the Republican regulars is a most significant fact, all
the same. "Dick Nixon is *our* kind of guy," is a phrase you
are very likely to hear when two or three or more of the
Republican party faithful are gathered together, and it is

the main reason why Nixon is, as of this writing, an easy favorite for the nomination.

Among the liberal intellectuals, on the other hand, dislike of Nixon is less a reasoned reaction than an allergy. William V. Shannon, liberal columnist for the liberal New York *Post*, has written: "Richard Nixon either offends one's taste, or he does not. If an individual has seen or heard Nixon perform a few times and still needs to have 'reasons' for rejecting him, that individual is obviously viewing the world with a different moral radar." These sentences reminded me vividly of the way a crusty old-school Republican crushed my sophomoric arguments in favor of the New Deal many years ago: "A man who does not dislike and distrust Franklin Roosevelt by instinct, without asking for reasons, is no gentleman."

The allergic dislike of Nixon is not confined to the liberals or the intellectuals. There is nothing benevolently neutral about the attitude toward him of the vast majority of regular Democrats, conservative as well as liberal. Speaker of the House Sam Rayburn has always disliked Nixon intensely—"That ugly fellow with the chinquapin eyes," he has called him. (An odd phrase—chinquapins are small edible brown nuts—but hardly a complimentary one.) Another leading old-guard Democrat invented the picturesque phrase, "lower than whale dung," to describe the Vice-President. The Democrats' Nixonophobia is not altogether politically motivated either, although of course Nixon has drawn a lot of Democratic blood in his political career. It is partly personal, too. "It's his Goddam holier-than-thou attitude that gets me down," one leading Senate Democrat has remarked. Another explained his dislike of Nixon by quoting the old jingle:

> *I do not like thee, Doctor Fell,*
> *The reason why I cannot tell,*
> *But this I know and know full well,*
> *I do not like thee, Doctor Fell.*

There are Republican Nixonophobes, too. Harold Stassen is one, of course. Chief Justice Earl Warren, who called Earl Mazo a "liar" to his face for his carefully factual and objective book on Nixon, without having read the book, is another. So is, or was, another former Republican governor of California, Goodwin Knight. Knight is said now to have made his peace with Nixon. But he had no peace in his heart when I first talked to him on the eve of the 1956 Republican convention in San Francisco. Knight was still, together with the egregious Stassen, fighting Nixon's vice-presidential nomination. This was a totally illogical endeavor, since any fool (except possibly Stassen) could see that nothing on earth could stop Nixon. But when I talked to him, it was quickly obvious that Knight's stand was not based on logic. It was based on sheer bile. Although he had never set eyes on me before, nothing whatever that Knight said to me about Nixon in a long interview was repeatable on paper, despite the old rule that it is impossible to libel a politician.

Nowadays, partly because of the actuarial risk that Nixon might at any moment become President, there is more discretion about him than there used to be, especially among Republicans, but Nixon still has plenty of Republican enemies lurking in the underbrush. Some are people who, like Knight or Warren, have known Nixon at firsthand for a long time, and some are even his ostensible political supporters.

And yet the old wisecrack about Thomas E. Dewey, often attributed to Alice Roosevelt Longworth—"You have to know him really well in order *really* to dislike him"—simply does not apply to Nixon. Those who know him really well (like Mrs. Longworth) are quite apt to like and admire him very much. Aside from his personal friend Attorney General William Rogers, his warmest admirers in the Eisenhower cabinet are Secretary of State Christian Herter and Secretary of Labor James Mitchell, both honorable, intelligent, and perceptive men whose "moral radar" is in excellent working order.

Among journalists, the Dewey rule has worked in reverse. In 1952 and immediately thereafter, the vast majority of reporters were anti-Nixon—most of them would have subscribed to Adlai Stevenson's description of Nixon as a "white-collar McCarthy." This is no longer true. There are still plenty of bitter anti-Nixonites among journalists, but they are largely concentrated among those who do not know him. One of the most devastating and seemingly perceptive anti-Nixon articles to appear in a national magazine, for example, was written by a well-known journalist who had never bothered to ask for an interview with his subject. Among reporters who have taken the trouble to get to know the Vice-President, the majority, including those (like this reporter) who were initially strongly hostile to Nixon, have found themselves according him an often grudging respect and admiration.

This is no doubt in part because most political reporters are interested in politics, presumably for the same reason that most baseball writers are interested in baseball. As he himself once remarked, Nixon is a "political animal." Because this is so, and because he is a man with really first-rate mental equipment, listening to Nixon talk politics is as pleasurable to one interested in that subject as, say, watching a rejuvenated Joe DiMaggio perform at his best would be to an avid baseball fan. That is certainly one reason why Nixon, who got, on balance, a bad press in his first years as Vice-President, gets a notably good press now. Another is that he understands news and newspapermen. He never wraps himself in the American flag or orates in private. He talks to newspapermen about matters which interest newspapermen, notably the news.

Partly because he has been getting a better press than he used to, but also, and more importantly, because since 1954 he has quite consciously changed his political style, Nixon does not now arouse quite the same passions that he used to arouse. And yet his capacity to arouse passions is undoubted, and it has great political significance. The passionate admiration for Nixon among regular Republicans, the widespread feeling among them that he is "our kind of guy," could assure Nixon the nomination without a serious contest.

Nixon could not have aroused this admiration among the Republican regulars without being a thoroughly partisan politician, which he has been and still is, to the tips of his fingers and toes. The American people, as noted earlier, have been taught to regard the word "politician" as a pejorative word. In fact, a President who is not also an effective politician is a President who fails to perform one of his essential functions. But these days a great many people would rather vote for a presidential candidate who has the appearance, at least, of being "above politics." Thus Nixon's past partisanship, and his reputation as a tough professional politician, while an asset in the contest for the nomination, is no asset for the election. And if it comes to be widely believed that Nixon cannot win, then the Republican regulars in convention assembled may yet, with tears in many an eye, do what they have done before. They may choose the man they think can win over the man they most admire.

This is not the place to try to explain why Nixon has his mysterious capacity for arousing intensely admiring and intensely hostile emotions. Any attempt to do so involves both the case for Nixon and the case against Nixon, which will be examined later in this book. It is enough to note here that he does have this capacity, which Franklin Roosevelt had also, and that having it makes Nixon a unique figure on the contemporary political scene. The fact that he has his genius for attracting and repelling is deeply important to an understanding of the man, both as a human being and as a major political force.

The one fact that everybody knows about Nelson Rockefeller—that he is rich—is also deeply important to an understanding of Rockefeller.

Just how rich is Nelson Rockefeller? Nobody—not even Nelson Rockefeller—precisely knows. But this reporter's guess, which is a reasonably well-informed guess, is that Nelson Rockefeller, and all the other Rockefellers, are a great deal richer than they are generally supposed to be.

Some time ago, *Fortune* magazine estimated the personal fortunes of Nelson, his sister, Abby, and his four brothers at between one hundred and two hundred million dollars apiece, and the fortune of John D. Rockefeller, Jr., at between four and seven hundred million. That makes a minimum of over a billion, a maximum of under two billion. *Fortune* also estimated the value of all the Rockefeller charities at around a billion, for a grand total of Rockefeller-owned or Rockefeller-influenced money of between two and three billion dollars.

These are the generally accepted figures. I have never been made privy to the secret financial archives of the Rockefellers. But I should be prepared to eat my boots in béarnaise if those figures are not low. They may be very low indeed. Consider the following facts.

In the early 1900s, after the dissolution of the Standard Oil trust, old John D. Rockefeller toted up the value of his Standard holdings, in his usual precise way. The total came to exactly $815, 647, 796.89. This was quite aside from all personal and other possessions. By 1910 the Rockefeller fortune certainly topped nine hundred million dollars, according to the first John D.'s ablest biographer, Allan Nevins.

Now let us suppose that the reader's grandfather possessed a more easily imaginable fortune—let us lop off four zeros and call it $90,000. Let us suppose that this sum was invested with great care and foresight in 1910. Let us further suppose that since then the fortune has been managed with expert tenderness; that the tax bite has been held to a minimum, by prior distribution of the fortune before Grandpa's death and by other means; that much of the capital has been invested in oil, that most lucrative investment; and that much of the income has been reinvested rather than spent. Would not the reader be disappointed if the fortune came to a mere $200,000 or $300,000 today?

Indeed, would not a million or even two or three million seem a more reasonable figure, especially in view of the stock-market boom of recent years? If you want a notion of what the boom has done to the paper value of the holdings of the rich, consider the statistics in a rather fascinating article about the financial adventures of Laurance Rockefeller, Nelson's brother, which appeared in the *Wall Street Journal* in the summer of 1959. Laurance Rockefeller, since the war, has gone in for being a "venture capitalist," investing in comparatively risky undertakings with the hope and expectation of making big capital gains. He has done well. "Since the end of World War II," the *Journal* reporter wrote, presumably after a talk with Laurance, "Mr. Rockefeller has invested about $6,750,000 in some two dozen companies. At the end of 1958, these investments . . . were worth more than $28 million. *Had the money stayed in oil shares, the investment would have been worth about $23.5 million.*"

In other words, Laurance Rockefeller quadrupled his money by taking risks. But the money would have been more than tripled, in any case, if he had just let his money stay where it was—and tripled, not since 1910, but since 1945.

In short, if the Rockefeller fortune, both in personal investments and in charitable foundations, has only been doubled or tripled since that distant day when John D. added it up down to the last eighty-nine cents, then the Rockefeller fortune has been very badly managed. And that seems unlikely, which is why it is reasonable to suppose that the total Rockefeller fortune may well amount to several times the accepted figures of between one and two billion dollars. It would not be at all surprising, according to one reasonably expert guess, if all the Rockefeller family assets—all the Rockefeller-con-

trolled money as well as the Rockefeller-owned money—came
to something like ten billion dollars.

As a practical matter, of course, it would be impossible for
Nelson Rockefeller to estimate his fortune down to the eighty-
nine cents, and it might be difficult to estimate it down to
the last twenty million dollars. How, for example, are you to
put an exact price tag on Nelson Rockefeller's share of the
enormous heap of stone and steel called Rockefeller Center?
But whatever guess you wish to make of his total worth, the
fact remains that Nelson Rockefeller is immensely, stupen-
dously, redundantly rich.

He is the only potential presidential candidate in our history whose family's personal economic decisions might conceivably have an important national impact. (Averell Harriman, of course, is a very rich man, and so is Joseph Kennedy,
father of candidate Jack. But neither has anything approaching the vast economic power which the Rockefeller family is
collectively capable of exerting.) Because this is so, if the
Rockefeller-for-President boom does not die a-borning, the
Rockefeller fortune is dead certain to be a political issue, perhaps little mentioned but decisively important all the same,
like Jack Kennedy's Catholicism.

Aside from simple vastness, moreover, there are two ways
in which the Rockefeller fortune is a special kind of fortune.
From one point of view the Rockefellers are richer than they
seem. From another point of view they are not so rich.

The Rockefellers are richer than they seem, in the sense
that the vast capital aggregations of the Rockefeller Foundation and the infinite variety of other Rockefeller charities
add to the total power and influence of the family. This is
not to suggest, of course, that the finance committee of the
Rockefeller Foundation, for example, is going to use the
money at its disposal to forward Nelson Rockefeller's political
ambitions. But the charities must be weighed on the plus side

of the ledger, all the same, in any attempt to assess the political significance of the Rockefeller money.

Consider the 1958 New York election. "If Nelson makes it," a friend of his remarked in the homestretch, "he'll be the first man to ride to high office on a tide of philanthropy." There is not a single voting group which has not benefited in one way or another from the immense Rockefeller charities—indeed, there is hardly an American citizen who has not so benefited. Nelson Rockefeller himself, either through his International Basic Economy Corporation or through his private charities, had been actively involved in building low-cost housing in Puerto Rico, improving the economy of Israel, and creating educational opportunities for Negroes—which certainly did him no harm with the Puerto Ricans, the Jews, and the Negroes. The advantage was the greater because the name of Rockefeller's opponent, also a rich man, was connected with no charity. "Ever hear of a Harriman Foundation?" the taxi drivers asked.

Cynics have contended that the Rockefeller charities were planned that way, to make the family popular with all possible economic and social groups. This is not true, or only partly true. But it is certainly true that Nelson Rockefeller's money has enabled him to give expression to his interest in public affairs in a manner no ordinary politician could afford. Beginning in 1956, for example, he and his brothers subsidized, at a cost of several hundred thousand dollars, a series of "Rockefeller reports" on such subjects as the national defense, education, and the national economy. The reports, which synthesized the thinking of panels of distinguished experts, got a lot of favorable attention and did not hurt Rockefeller a bit in his bid for the governorship. Moreover, the experts hired for the Rockefeller reports or for such other Rockefeller charities as the Government Affairs Foundation provide Rockefeller with a ready-made brains trust.

It is in such ways that the Rockefeller family is richer in

terms of power and influence than even the vast fortunes of
the family would suggest. But there is another way in which
a Rockefeller—an individual Rockefeller, like Nelson—is not
as rich as he seems. For the Rockefeller fortune is above all a
family fortune. Nelson's private fortune, like those of his
four brothers and his sister, is inextricably involved in the
Rockefeller family fortune. In this sense, it is not his to do
with as he pleases. And a man whose money is not his, to do
with as he pleases, is not as rich as he seems.

The fact that Nelson Rockefeller's money is in a sense not
his is a fact of considerable political significance. In a conversation with one of the very few men who are privy to the
real facts about the Rockefeller family fortune, I once pointed
out that if Nelson made a serious try for the presidency, things
were dead sure to get a bit rough. Even when Rockefeller had
been a mere Assistant Secretary of State there had been whispers that his political views had been influenced by the great
Rockefeller financial holdings in South America. The whispers
were untrue, of course. But any serious presidential aspirant
automatically generates pitiless opposition. There were sure
to be whispers—perhaps shouts—that Rockefeller was a pris-
oner of "the interests," including his own interests, just as
there were whispers that Jack Kennedy was "controlled by
the Pope."

To all this the man I was interviewing easily assented. Considering how great was the prize at stake, I said, might it not
be wise for Rockefeller to consider divesting himself of all
his interests, voluntarily selling out, as former Secretary of
Defense Charles Wilson had finally done involuntarily, and
putting all his assets into cash or bonds?

A look of genuine consternation came over the face of
my interlocutor. "Look," he said, when he had recovered his
breath, "there is just no way on earth to de-Rockefeller a
Rockefeller."

He was right, of course. It would be impossible for Rockefeller to liquidate his holdings without terrible legal, economic, and family complications. But the fact remains that the vast Rockefeller fortune is sure to influence heavily Nelson Rockefeller's political future. Is the fortune a political plus or a political minus?

In the 1958 gubernatorial campaign, the money was unquestionably an asset. Leonard Hall, one of his competitors for the nomination, once ruefully described to me the effect of the Rockefeller name: "We politicians get to be pretty good at smiling and shaking hands—hell, that's our business. But Nelson would go upstate and smile and shake hands with some leader's wife, and she'd get all watery at the knees, like he was a prince or something." In this sense the Rockefeller name, which was probably the most hated name in America fifty years ago, is no doubt an asset. It is an asset not only because the charities have made it an admired name but also simply because the name is known. One of the great problems for any presidential aspirant is simply to impinge on the consciousness of what the late Frank Kent used to call "the great rancid American people." The names of Hubert Humphrey, Stuart Symington, even Lyndon Johnson mean little or nothing to a vast proportion of the voters. That problem is largely solved for Rockefeller, for there are very few people who have not heard his name.

Being a Rockefeller is an asset in another way as well, of course. As Rockefeller has frankly acknowledged, without a great deal of money he could not support the vast number of "studies"—public-opinion polls, analyses of issues, and the like—which he constantly orders. Moreover, in his office in Rockefeller Center, Nelson Rockefeller already had, long before he became governor, the nucleus of a campaign organization, with everything a candidate needs, from astute political and public relations advisers to plenty of stenographers to assure that all letters are promptly answered.

For the rest, there are those who argue that the Rockefeller money is an asset, not because it will be improperly used but simply because it exists. According to this theory, the very large number of influential people whose financial fortunes are bound up in one way or another with the Rockefeller economic empire will support Rockefeller, as it were, by instinct, without being subjected to any pressure whatsoever.

But if the Rockefeller money is an asset in this and other ways, there are certain ways in which it is not an asset. Again, one returns to the analogy with Kennedy's Catholicism. The evidence suggests that being a Catholic is a net political asset to a candidate on the state level. There are certainly a great many Protestants who would unhesitatingly vote for a Catholic for senator or governor, as the remarkably large number of incumbent Catholic senators and governors clearly proves. But some, at any rate, of these same people (nobody can possibly guess how many) would have sufficient lingering religious prejudices so that they would balk at the thought of a Catholic in the White House. By the same token, while Rockefeller's wealth was certainly an asset in the New York election, there are unquestionably some voters (again, nobody can possibly guess how many) who would balk at the notion of so classic a capitalist occupying the White House.

The fact that Rockefeller is a Republican as well as a capitalist further complicates the equation. There is one phrase which a feeler of the people's pulse hears over and over again, and which represents the great central asset of the Democratic party: "The Republicans are for the big guy, and the Democrats are for the little guy."—by which is meant, of course, that the Republicans are for the rich and the Democrats for the poor. It is because this view is so remarkably widely held that it is much more difficult, as Nelson Rockefeller is well aware, for a very "big guy" like himself to succeed in politics as a Republican than as a Democrat.

In sum, the Rockefeller money must probably be listed on balance as a political asset—but a dubious asset, an asset on which he cannot strongly count. Although his name is known, to most people it still means "money," and not much more. If Rockefeller is ever to reach the White House—whether in 1960, in 1964, or even thereafter—the name is going to have to come to mean a good deal more than that.

In all these ways, at any rate, the fact that everybody knows about Rockefeller—that he is very rich—is politically a most significant fact. It is an even more significant fact in a human sense.

Being immensely, famously, fabulously rich is a most unusual experience, after all. It sets a man apart from other people, like having been badly wounded in a war or having conquered the drug habit. Although it has its obvious compensations, it cannot be an altogether agreeable experience. I once suggested to Rockefeller that it must be a bit like having an enormous nose or some other visible physical deformity, and he did not dispute the suggestion. People who meet Nelson Rockefeller are always aware of the dollar sign that floats conspicuously if invisibly above his head. It is there, but one must not mention it.

Having that invisible dollar sign hovering over his head tends to hedge a very rich man off from his fellows, as divinity doth hedge a king. And this suggests why Rockefeller so visibly and obviously enjoys himself in his new role as a triumphantly successful tribune of the people. For politics gives a man like Rockefeller a means to overleap the wall of money which separates a very rich man from other people.

After he was nominated for governor in 1958, Rockefeller described how, when he was supposed to be resting at his place in Maine, he took off in an old car with his son Steve and drove about in upstate New York, talking to people and trying to get the feel of what they were thinking. "It was a fascinating experience," Rockefeller told me. "Of course I'd never done anything like it before—never had a reason to, an excuse. There was one man, for example, he'd lost his job with the New York Central and he had his mother to support, and he told me he didn't know what he was going to do, where to turn. Well, that man wasn't a statistic on the unemployment rolls, he was a human being. Until you get out and talk to people that way, you feel kind of cut off, separated from reality."

The experience of being "cut off, separated from reality," by vast amounts of money is an experience which leaves its mark upon a man. It explains a lot about Nelson Rockefeller. It at least partly explains the frenetic, driving ambition which Rockefeller has displayed since he was a boy, and which seems at first glance an irrational characteristic in a man who already has all the worldly advantages that the most ambitious man might aspire to.

Wallace Harrison, architect for Rockefeller Center and one of the handful of men who know Rockefeller really well, tells the story of a harrowing trip up from New York to Maine in the *Dragon Lady*, a former subchaser Rockefeller bought after the war. The passengers were mostly Dartmouth classmates of Rockefeller, bent on a reunion, and the destination was Seal Harbor, Rockefeller's summer place on the Maine coast. The voyage had been a very rough one, with two really dangerous storms, and Seal Harbor was still a long way to go.

Everyone was exhausted except Rockefeller, who was more exuberant and energetic than ever in his new role as sea dog. The captain, a professional sailor and down-Easter called Henry Conary, hopefully approached Harrison and asked: "Think he'll let us turn in and get a little sleep?" Knowing Rockefeller, Harrison replied that it was far more likely that Rockefeller would insist on pressing on to Seal Harbor. Conary then asked the question which has puzzled a lot of people who have known Nelson Rockefeller:

"What's a-pepperin' the guy anyway?"

A good many things are a-pepperin' Nelson Rockefeller, as we shall see, but being rich is certainly one of them. Most rich men who have inherited really gigantic fortunes share certain characteristics in common (so do men who have themselves made gigantic fortunes, but the characteristics are different). They have a certain caution—they have so much to lose. They also have a certain inner confidence—they are accustomed to getting what they want. And most men who have inherited a great deal of money want above all to excel, to prove themselves on their own. Harold Vanderbilt wanted to excel, among other things, at bridge, and Henry du Pont at collecting American art and furniture. Contract and Winterthur are their lasting memorials. Averell Harriman wanted to excel at everything, from polo to politics, and he very nearly succeeded. And the same urge to prove that he is not only a Rockefeller but a man, and an able man, is doubtless a-pepperin' Nelson Rockefeller.

Even if he had not been rich, one suspects, even if his name had been Smith and he had been born penniless, Nelson Rockefeller would have ended up in politics, for politics is in his blood. One old political pro, watching Rockefeller perform in his first political campaign in the autumn of 1958, remarked admiringly: "God must have meant Nelson to be a politician." But a Nelson Rockefeller born without a penny under the name of Smith would have been a different sort of politician—perhaps a good deal more conservative, for example—and a very different sort of human being. That is why the one thing everybody knows about Rockefeller—that he is rich—is an important thing to know.

As for Nixon, a number of his classmates wrote me that he was the "last man" they would have expected to become a leading politician—which is rather odd, since Nixon in his school and college days was forever running for office and getting elected. But Nixon might very well have ended up as a successful lawyer rather than as a politician. At one time he considered joining John Foster Dulles's old law firm, Sullivan and Cromwell—he decided against it in the end be-

cause he thought he would be lost as a junior clerk in one of
the huge New York law factories. If he had decided otherwise
one can be reasonably certain that he would have become a
senior partner before his time, and that he would have become very rich and very successful indeed.

Nixon went into politics at least partly by accident and at
least partly because it seemed a good way for an ambitious
young lawyer to get ahead after the war. He went ahead
very fast indeed—Vice-President in his thirties, leading presidential candidate in his forties. He could not possibly have
gone ahead so fast if he had not had those qualities which
make him one of today's few "controversial" politicians, the
qualities that make people admire him extravagantly or dislike him intensely. That is why the one thing all Americans
know about Nixon—whether they like him or not—is also important. With his ambition and ability, Nixon would no doubt
in time have made his mark in politics in any case. But without his capacity for arousing strong emotions he, too, would
have been a different kind of politician, and a different kind
of man.

So much then for the two important things that everybody
knows about Nixon and Rockefeller. Now let us have a look
at these two men in their outward seeming—the way they look
and talk and act, the way they appear, not to a close friend
(for this writer is not a close friend of either man and could
not write this book if he were) but to someone who has talked
with them both at length and who has often observed them
in action.

3

What Are They Like?

If you had an appointment with Vice-President Nixon in Washington, you would probably meet him either at his house or in one of his two offices on Capitol Hill. None of these three backgrounds is particularly elaborate or impressive. The Vice-President's office in the Senate Office Building is like any senator's. His office in the Capitol itself is hardly more than a hideaway—in its smallness and plainness it provides a sharp contrast to the plush and expensive suite newly acquired by Majority Leader Lyndon Johnson. If visitors note the contrast, and comment on it, Nixon doesn't mind a bit.

As for the house, it is a fairly large, totally undistinguished fieldstone house, with a big pleasant porch overlooking Rock Creek Park. It has been described as being in the "fashionable" part of Washington. "Respectable" would be more accurate (Georgetown is the only part of Washington which can really lay claim to high fashion). Nixon's neighbors are for the most part reasonably prosperous lawyers, businessmen, and the like.

Whether you met Nixon at home or in one of his offices, you would be greeted politely but with a certain reserve. Nixon is absolutely lacking in the warmth of manner—which often has no more real meaning than a facial tic—of the majority of big-time politicians. He also wholly lacks the ability to make small talk. He tries to talk small occasionally, about golf (his golf form is described as "horrible" but he plays with so ferocious a will to win that he often makes a respectable score) or about football (he really likes watching football) or the weather or the like. But his heart is not in it. Such things do not really interest him. What interests him is politics. Politics is his one true love.

The word is used in its larger sense, to include the whole process of government, and the great national and international issues involved in that process, as well as the vote-catching maneuvers and the bureaucratic power struggles also involved in the process. If you were not prepared to talk about one aspect or another of this large subject your appointment with the Vice-President would probably be brief.

When talking about his favorite subject, Nixon talks extremely well, which is one reason, as we have seen, why he gets a better press than he once did. Most of his sentences (in sharp contrast to President Eisenhower's) are capable of being parsed, even when he is talking completely off the cuff and before an audience of one. Indeed, there is an oddly academic flavor to much of Nixon's conversation. He visibly thinks as he talks—occasionally he puts his hand to his forehead, as though attempting by that gesture to rearrange his thoughts. His other favorite gesture is a palms-down chopping or waving motion with his hands, with his elbows held close to his sides.

As for the substance of his talk, that depends on the audience and the occasion. When he was visited in the summer of 1959 by Soviet First Deputy Premier Frol Kozlov, Nixon subsequently remarked that Kozlov was "extremely intelligent, capable, and equipped with a facility essential to the politician—that of appearing to answer a question emphatically when, in reality, the whole point of the question has been successfully evaded." The remark is revealing, for when he prefers to evade "the whole point" of some question, Nixon is well equipped with that "facility essential to the politician." But he can also be quite remarkably candid, which is another reason his stock has steadily risen with most reporters.

Nixon has one habit I have never found in any other politician. Talking with a journalist, he will quite often reverse the roles, so that he becomes the interviewer and the journalist the interviewee. If the subject is one which particularly interests him, and the journalist has some facts about it which are new to him, Nixon will get out a big yellow lawyer's scratch pad and begin making extensive notes in a personal shorthand.

Nixon has the kind of inquiring, absorptive mind and the natural bump of curiosity which would have made him, one suspects, a very successful journalist. It has helped make him a successful politician. Before all his trips abroad, he demands very complete briefings from the State Department and the Central Intelligence Agency. Remarkably few politicians are good listeners, and at first the briefing officials were prepared for the glassy eyes and half-stifled yawns most politicians display when forced briefly to listen to voices other than their own. But they quickly learned to take their briefings of Nixon seriously. "He sure does his homework," one intelligence official has remarked, "and if you don't know the real answer when he asks a question, it's a lot better to say so."

This habit of doing his homework has served Nixon well.

Before his trip to Russia in the summer of 1959, Nixon spent weeks preparing himself for what was to come. In a sense, indeed, the famous debate in the kitchen of the model house at the fair was not really unrehearsed, for Nixon had insisted on a very careful study of the Soviet propaganda line in all its aspects, and the best counterarguments against it. Even Nixon's bitterest critics agreed that he performed usefully in Russia, and his standing thereafter in the public-opinion polls shot upward.

There are other ways in which Nixon's ability to listen and his knack for knowing what is really going on have served him well. He does not, however, listen to what does not interest him. His manner of terminating an interview is quick and decisive. He simply gets up, opens the door of his office, and holds out his hand. Sometimes, if there is a point he wishes particularly to emphasize, he will continue the conversation for a little while at the door. More often, the parting is as polite—and as reserved—as the greeting.

So much for the face Nixon shows to the casual visitor, and to the world at large. Is it a pleasant face, an attractive face?

To try first to answer that question in its literal sense, Nixon is not, by most standards, a handsome man. People who dislike him without being able to explain why are as likely as not to refer to "those jowls." The jowls, with an assist from the beetling brows, have been a useful anti-Nixon symbol, especially for cartoonists like the brilliant Herblock, just as Dewey's mustache was a useful anti-Dewey symbol in 1948,[1] but unlike the mustache, the jowls are not removable. Nixon has aged a good deal, especially since 1956—his hairline has receded with alarming rapidity and the lines between his eyes and the corners of his mouth, which are faintly discernible

[1] *There are those who seriously contend that Dewey's mustache cost him the election and should thus rank with Samson's hair among history's most decisive hirsute adornments.*

even in college photographs, are now very deep. Nixon now looks, in fact, like a middle-aged Black Irishman, which is, in essence, what he is. But male beauty has not been a traditional qualification for the presidency, as a glance at any collection of presidential portraits suggests.

The reaction to the Nixon personality can only be wholly subjective, of course. There are those who have been strongly and unexpectedly impressed by him on first contact. A group of British journalists who dined with him informally some time ago thereafter sang his praises in somewhat extravagant terms. This was partly, as one of them has said, because they had expected a rancid and semi-literate reactionary and were surprised to find instead a man of obvious intelligence, perfectly willing to listen with a seemingly open mind to those who disagreed with him. Others, who have expected to dislike him very much, have disliked him very much. For what it is worth, I have always found a talk with Nixon not only a professionally rewarding experience but a personally agreeable one. This is in part, no doubt, because I share his passion for politics. But it is also pleasant for one whose trade involves talking to a lot of politicians to talk to one who never orates to an audience of one and who is quite incapable of slapping a back. In short, I find Nixon not only an interesting but a likable human being.

And yet I can understand why some people do not find him likable. There is something mechanical, something faintly inhuman about the man, as there is about Dewey, whom he resembles in a number of ways. There is something of the too perfect quality of the very handsome girl, whose hair is always in place, whose slip never shows—and who is never led to the altar.

Nixon's supporters and admirers are aware of this faintly inhuman quality, which tends to make Nixon a cardboard figure, two-dimensional. "If only we could get Dick to take up some kind of messy hobby, like chicken raising," one

Nixon man mused some time ago, only half jokingly. "Then we could get pictures of him messing around with his chickens, in an old tweed coat with a button off, maybe smoking a pipe."

Nixon is quite aware that, in the current cant of the pseudo-science of public-opinion analysis, the "image" he "projects" lacks warmth. But, as he sensibly says, "There are some things you can't do anything about. You've got to be what you are, you can't pretend to be something different." It is thus quite unlikely that Nixon will take up chicken raising or take any other measures to disguise the reserve which makes it impossible for him to act the "buddy-buddy boy."

Nixon is not only reserved. He is also oddly impersonal about himself. When asked to talk about himself, as in the conversation published in the appendix of this book, he talks easily (far more so than Rockefeller) and quite dispassionately, as though he were some disembodied observer, regarding the phenomenon, Richard Nixon, through an interested but by no means uncritical eye.

Nowadays, indeed, when Nixon is talking in private, it is hard to picture him as a "ruthless partisan . . . a politician who divides and embitters people," as he was once described, at the time with reason, by Walter Lippmann. Some Rip van Winkle, unaware of Nixon's political history, would probably come away from a private talk with Nixon with the impression that here was a rather judicial-minded fellow, a bit academic in manner, highly articulate but at the same time reserved to the point of shyness.

And Nixon is shy, difficult as it is to believe that such an adjective can be accurately applied to the most aggressive of living American politicians. As we shall see, shyness is the quality which most of his college and law-school classmates recall about the Nixon they used to know. It is an unexpected quality to find in a man with Nixon's reputation, but it is there all the same, and it is important to understand that it is there.

No one has ever called Nelson Rockefeller shy. And although the two men are alike in more ways than appear on the surface, the surface impression Rockefeller conveys is totally different from Nixon's. Rockefeller's manner has a warmth and friendliness which Nixon is quite incapable of displaying. Some persons, indeed, find Rockefeller's manner a trifle *too* warm and friendly. His normal greeting to a male acquaintance is a hearty "Hi, fella," and he is as likely as not to put an affectionate arm around a new acquaintance's shoulder—something Nixon is incapable of doing.

In manner, in fact, the scion of stupendous wealth is far more a tribune of the people than the poor storekeeper's son with his *noli me tangere* reserve. It is easy to see why Rockefeller was one of the most popular boys in his class at Dartmouth thirty years ago, and indeed many of his mannerisms, like the "hi, fella" and the arm on the shoulder, are the mannerisms of the Dartmouth of that era. And it is still easy to visualize Rockefeller as a Dartmouth undergraduate. He looks a good deal younger than his fifty-one years. ("Wealth preserves," a wag has remarked, paraphrasing Lord Acton, "and great wealth preserves absolutely.") Until rather recently, he used to dress as though he were still in Dartmouth—his shoes, particularly, had that down-at-heel, never-been-shined college look. Nowadays he is a good deal more natty, as befits a governor of the Empire State—he goes in especially for double-breasted suits. But he still has a certain rumpled look which reminds some people of Wendell Willkie. The rumpled look also provides a contrast with Nixon who, like Dewey, is quite incapable of looking anything but neat as a new pin, even in a sport shirt.

Rockefeller, most people would agree, is a better-looking man than Nixon. At least Rockefeller has a more presidential look—he has a strong face, jut-jawed, with a biggish nose, all his hair, and no glasses. His eyes are by all odds the most striking feature of his face. They are somewhat hooded, and long and narrow at either end, so that they have a faintly oriental look. To those who know him well, Rockefeller's odd eyes are a barometer of his moods. One who knows him well is Thomas W. Braden, publisher of a California newspaper, the Oceanside *Blade-Tribune,* who has been a younger friend of Rockefeller's for some years.

In an article for his newspaper, after describing Rockefeller's charm and "niceness," Braden continues: "Rockefeller is not merely 'nice.' In his second layer he is tough, and people who have had occasion to cross him in private dealings have been made immediately aware that he can be very tough indeed. . . . You might notice the toughness of Nelson Rockefeller in a curious narrowing of the eyes when he thinks someone is trying to take advantage of him, or is thinking of him solely for his money, or when things are going wrong, and someone suggests what he is working on might fail."

Despite the odd eyes, Rockefeller's face is friendly, open, and boyish. It is the kind of face children instinctively like, and it is quite obvious to anyone who has seen him with large numbers of them that Rockefeller genuinely likes children, which may be the reason they like him. In his campaign for governor, Rockefeller had a notable Pied Piper effect on children, just as President Eisenhower did in his two campaigns. Being a Pied Piper with children may have a certain political significance, despite the legal voting age. Adlai Stevenson and Averell Harriman are both non-Pied Pipers. So, for that matter, is Richard Nixon.

Rockefeller is built like a football guard, although in college he played soccer, perhaps because his parents feared a football-playing Rockefeller would attract too much attention. He has the fierce physical energy which often goes with a stocky frame and which is an enormous, almost an essential, asset to a politician. The man is, and always has been, a study in perpetual motion—he is in such a permanent hurry that he sometimes seems on the point of breaking into a trot. He pauses often, as he charges about the hideous old state house at Albany, to shout a greeting, give an order, put a friendly arm over a shoulder or laugh at a joke, but then he is off again, relentlessly, restlessly on the move. A friend who worked with him in the wartime days recalls the experience as "the most exhausting I've ever had. It wasn't just that the hours were long, though Lord knows they were—it was the intensity Nelson brought to the job."

The intensity shows itself in his conversation. His talk on almost any subject is animated and enthusiastic, and when he wants to persuade it takes on a missionary fervor. Like President Eisenhower, he is an unabashed user of clichés (this is true of almost any successful politician—one of Adlai Stevenson's greatest weaknesses as a politician has been a terror of clichés). Rockefeller likes to talk about general ideas, and about his job, which he obviously enjoys as he has enjoyed nothing before in his life. But he does not much like to talk about himself—he has none of Nixon's ability to look at himself with an interested but impersonal eye. And when certain subjects are introduced—notably his presidential plans and ambitions, there is apt to be that "curious narrowing of the eyes" and a sudden quiet caution.

Rockefeller has few mannerisms. He is likely to sit with his arm over the side of a chair, his hands quietly clasped, except when he uses them to emphasize a point or to run his fingers through his hair. He does have certain small eccentricities. He has a passion for rearranging objects. Even in a perfect stranger's house, he will instantly march up to a crooked picture on the wall and straighten it, and he has been known to rearrange all the furniture in a friend's living room, as it were, absent-mindedly. One beautiful and witty lady remembers being somewhat miffed when, during a tête-à-tête dinner, he seemed more interested in achieving a more artistic arrangement of the table flowers than in her sprightly conversation. He also has an odd passion for changing the landscape about—he has been known to have large trees and even small forests uprooted and replanted nearer to his heart's desire. He has, in short, something very like a compulsion to impose order and balance on his surroundings.

He has other peculiarities. Although far healthier than most horses, he is a pill lover. He always carries a large supply of pills, and since he hardly ever needs a pill himself, he prescribes them in large quantities for the ailments of acquaintances. (Oddly, his medical ministrations are generally effective.) He is also completely incapable of spelling correctly, a family failing (on both sides) which he admits cheerfully and even with something of the quiet pride with which tone-deaf people acknowledge their defect.

Yet, despite these minor eccentricities, the impression Rockefeller conveys is one of healthy, self-confident, exuberant, likable normality. If such a thing is possible, he seems an abnormally normal man. That is the impression he has always conveyed, since he was a very young man.

This almost abnormal normality of Rockefeller's is likely to be one of the first things to impress new acquaintances. "Why," they say, "he's just as comfortable as an old shoe." The other thing that impresses those who meet him is how "nice" he is. Nice is a vague word, hard to define precisely, but whatever quality it describes, to the great majority of people Rockefeller has that quality. His niceness is underlined and accentuated, moreover, by the fact that he is so rich. Most people somehow expect that a man rich beyond the dreams of avarice will be a chilly snob. When they find instead that the rich man has a big warm smile and that his manner is as comfortable as an old shoe, they are apt to "get all watery at the knees, like he was a prince or something."

Not everybody, by any means, likes Nelson Rockefeller, as we shall see. But there is no doubt at all that he is and always has been, to the great majority of people who have had any contact with him, an extraordinarily likable man.

And this likableness, this niceness, is Rockefeller's major asset as far as the Republican nomination is concerned. Indeed, aside from the built-in advantage of being the governor of the biggest state in the union, it is almost his only real asset. His money, as previously noted, is a doubtful political asset, if it is an asset at all. In political experience, he is no equal to Nixon. He is regarded as a pretty dubious Republican by a great many Republican regulars, and they will go on preferring Nixon whatever efforts Rockefeller may make to prove that he is indeed a "real Republican." But that niceness of Rockefeller's, that likableness which impresses almost everyone who meets him, is an asset to reckon with.

"Dick Nixon's got the same trouble I have," Thomas E. Dewey once remarked rather disarmingly to a reporter. "Too many people don't like us both." Nixon is quite aware of this "trouble," of course. As he remarked in the revealing interview in the appendix of this book: "It depends on what the times call for. If the time comes when the Republican party and the voters are looking for an outwardly warm, easygoing, gregarious type, then they will not want the sort of man I am."

Nixon might have been describing Rockefeller, although he almost certainly did not have him in mind when he spoke. It is in this sense that Rockefeller's niceness, his likableness, is an important political factor. For whatever the quality is that makes a first-rate political campaigner, Rockefeller has it. He proved that in the autumn of 1958 in his first campaign for political office.

As Rockefeller moves about in a crowd, coatless and tieless, often with his sleeves rolled up over muscular forearms and with his hair tousled, he visibly displays three politically priceless characteristics. One is that huge grin—one of his supporters has called it a "Gee, I like you" smile. Another is a quality of vitality and exuberance which makes working for Rockefeller "an exhausting experience," but which also pleases and impresses a crowd. A third is the indefinable

ability to project "sincerity." Rockefeller is no great shakes as
an orator, and when he says the inevitable "few words" they
are rarely profound. But after he has grinned his last big grin
and waved his last cheerful wave from his departing limou-
sine, you can almost always hear someone in the crowd mur-
muring, "He's so sincere," or "You just can't help liking him."
Those phrases are the accolade of a great campaigner.

If Rockefeller can "project" this remarkably effective "image" nationwide, he may even begin to look like a probable
winner. If Nixon also looks like a probable winner, Rockefeller certainly will not become President of the United States
—not in 1960, at any rate. But if, as the crucial moment ap-
proaches, Nixon begins to look like a probable loser, then
Rockefeller may have a chance. He may even have a very
good chance—on that point the reader, with his advantage in
time over the writer, is in a better position to judge.

So much, at any rate, for the superficial impression which
Nixon and Rockefeller convey—so much for their outer carapace. It is an interesting exercise to try to understand a little
about how the carapace was formed and what lies beneath it.

4

Nixon in Crisis

There have been three occasions in Nixon's career when he might have been destroyed. On two of these occasions he might have been destroyed politically—which might have been, to a man of Nixon's totally political temperament, a personal disaster short only of death itself. On the third occasion it was death itself that Nixon faced. The way he reacted to these moments of great danger tells a lot about the man beneath the carapace.

Nixon first came face to face with political destruction during the 1952 campaign, when he was Eisenhower's running mate for the first time, and when, in September, charges that he was the beneficiary of a "secret millionaires' fund" suddenly exploded in his face. The famous fund crisis was one of the most extraordinary episodes in American political his-

tory, and Nixon's course during the crisis gave him a claim
to a place among American history's most extraordinary politicians. A book—and a rather fascinating one—could be devoted to the whole story of the five days of the fund crisis.
Here I shall describe those highlights of the story which cast
light on the kind of man Nixon was and is. I shall concentrate
especially on the way Nixon chose to deal with the head of
his ticket, General Eisenhower, an aspect of the story which
is remarkably revealing and which has never before been
fully told.

But first to set the stage. Nixon was thirty-nine at the time.
He had been in politics only six years. He had been chosen as
General Eisenhower's running mate largely through Dewey's
influence. He was chosen for the sort of reasons for which
Vice-Presidents are traditionally chosen. He was acceptable
to the Taft wing of the party. As a Californian, he came from
a key state where the failure of Governor Earl Warren's candidacy might cost the ticket votes. As a westerner, he might
take a bit of the curse off the largely eastern coloration of the
Eisenhower movement. And his role in bringing Alger Hiss
to justice made him an impeccable anti-Communist, thus giving the ticket some reinsurance against the defection of Senator Joseph McCarthy's admirers. In short, Nixon was at the
beginning of the fund crisis thoroughly in the Throttlebottom
tradition. After the crisis was over, he was a major politician,
as he has been ever since—much admired, much hated, but
no Throttlebottom.

When the storm over the fund broke, on Thursday, September 18, 1952, Nixon was whistle-stopping in northern
California. On board his campaign train were two people
who have had a profound influence on his career. One was
his wife, Pat, whom Nixon met in 1937 at a tryout for a Little
Theater play, proposed to that very night in an uncharacter-
istically impulsive moment, and married in 1940. Like Nixon
himself, Pat Nixon is not easy to know well. Like Nixon, she

is said to have a rare but furious temper, although her usual manner is coolly competent. She shares other characteristics with Nixon—a good intelligence, much energy, and a strong ambition. At one time—after the 1954 campaign—she almost changed the course of American political history by persuading Nixon to withdraw from politics to go into law practice. Otherwise, she has been a major political asset to Nixon. She has acted as a sort of extra backbone for a man whose backbone already had great tensile strength, magnifying and intensifying those qualities, like his drive and ambition, which he already had in abundance.

The second of these two people who have deeply influenced Nixon's career was Murray Chotiner. Chotiner was a part-time political adviser for Nixon in his 1946 campaign for Congress against Jerry Voorhis. He was Nixon's campaign manager in 1950, when he beat Helen Gahagan Douglas for the Senate, and again in 1952. Chotiner is, or was, a remarkable political phenomenon in his own right. He managed victorious campaigns for Warren and Knowland, as well as Nixon, and he has often been described as a political genius. Of all California's strange tribe of professional campaign managers—brought into existence by California's peculiar and now defunct cross-filing system and by the state's penchant for popular referendums—Chotiner was probably the most successful, except perhaps for the redoubtable Whittaker and Baxter.

If Nixon can be said to have had a political mentor, it was Chotiner, and he is therefore worth a brief glance. In 1956, still unproved charges that Chotiner had tried to use his political connections, including his connections with Nixon, to get favors for his law clients transformed him—at least for the time being—from a major political asset in California into something like political poison. Since then, Nixon and Chotiner have had no political relationship. But Nixon, to his credit, is still outspokenly loyal to Chotiner, and he considers it a "tragedy" that Chotiner became involved in "the kind of law business which does not mix well with politics." As this is written Chotiner is planning to run for Congress, partly in order to prove that he is not political poison now. If he is as shrewd a manager of himself as he was as the manager of California's Big Three, his opponent is to be pitied.

Chotiner is not only shrewd—he is also a rather agreeable fellow with a somewhat cynical wit. He has a distinctly southern California air about him—when I first met him, I was impressed by his white silk tie, his dove-gray suit, and his enormous cuff links, which turned out on closer inspection to be miniature watches. Like Nixon, he has one true love, and that is politics. But in Chotiner's case the word has a decidedly limited definition. To him, politics is the art of winning elections. Talking to him, one senses that as far as he is concerned there really is nothing more to politics—the issues, for example, are of interest only in that they may help or hinder a candidate in his single mission of attracting votes on Election Day. As we shall see, an important part of the case against Nixon is that for too long a time he, too, regarded winning elections as a politician's chief function.

Amazingly, the astute Chotiner, who knew all about the fund, never smelled the terrible political danger in it. Nor did Attorney General-to-be William Rogers nor Nixon's shrewd press secretary at the time, James Bassett, who were also on the train. Neither these men nor Nixon himself took the fund story very seriously at first. Nixon's first reaction was to say that he had been "smeared" by Communists. This reaction was in accordance with Chotiner's basic precept, laid down in a speech to the party faithful—"An attack is always a smear when it is directed to our own candidates." Thus Nixon and his clever advisers tended at first to dismiss as a mere pinprick what was in fact a knife thrust at the heart.

That none of them were worried by the fund story when it broke may be a reflection on their political sagacity or their sense of values, but it is certainly true. The fund had never been a secret—Dana Smith, a lawyer of remarkable candor and immense political naïveté, who was treasurer of the fund, had beat the more promising Republican bushes for money for the fund up and down the Coast. Everyone involved, on both the giving and receiving ends, had regarded the fund as a special sort of campaign fund—an out-of-season campaign fund, to be sure, but in no way reprehensible. When columnist Pete Edson had earlier asked Nixon about the fund, Nixon had casually given him Smith's telephone number and suggested that Edson get the details from him.

But by Sunday night, three days after the fund story had broken, Nixon and the men around him were well aware that the seeming pinprick might be a knife in the heart. The Washington *Post,* the New York *Herald Tribune,* and other papers had called for Nixon's resignation. Harold Stassen had sent him a long, pompous wire asking him to withdraw, and Nixon was well aware that some of the men to whom Eisenhower listened were also in favor of dumping him. He had himself thought seriously of withdrawing. But his wife, Pat, repeatedly said two things. "If you withdraw under fire," she said, "you will carry the scar for the rest of your life." And she said: "If you withdraw, Ike will lose."

Chotiner also maintained that Nixon's withdrawal would be interpreted as an admission of guilt and might defeat Eisenhower. And he insisted from the first that with proper management the crisis could be turned decisively to Nixon's advantage.

"I did what I always do," Nixon has said. "I considered all the worst alternatives, as cold-bloodedly as I could, and reached the analytical conclusion—that if I withdrew, Ike would probably lose. So I decided to make the effort to stay on, if possible with honor."

Although he has never said so, it is obvious in retrospect that Nixon reached another "analytical conclusion" as well—

that the key to his whole situation lay with Dwight D. Eisenhower. If he were not to be destroyed politically (and, in a sense, personally, too) the General must exonerate him completely. Nothing less would do. Moreover, Nixon must at all costs avoid being summoned for judgment, like a naughty little boy called into the parlor to be spanked or forgiven by an indulgent parent.

As soon as he realized that the storm was a real storm, and no mere teapot tempest, Nixon issued orders that he would under no circumstances speak to any spokesman for the General, but only to Eisenhower himself. The orders were quickly conveyed to the General's train. This was itself a bold move for the thirty-nine-year-old junior senator. Bolder moves were to follow.

Friday, Saturday, and Sunday passed without the expected telephone call from the General, who was under heavy conflicting pressures and who had said only that Nixon must be "as clean as a hound's tooth"—a remark which had, understandably, infuriated Nixon. At last, on Sunday night, while Nixon was in Portland, Oregon, the long-awaited call came through from the General in Missouri.

The way Nixon talked to the General—the revered conqueror of Hitler, who seemed then much more untouchably majestic than he came to seem later, when time and habit had whittled him down to human size—tells a lot about Nixon. One can well imagine another man, explaining in much self-justifying detail how the fund was essentially no different from any other campaign fund; how no contributor was allowed to give more than five hundred dollars; how every penny was regularly accounted for; and so on. But Nixon, amazingly, hardly mentioned the fund.

After some initial small talk, Nixon said that he would withdraw if the General—and the Republican National Committee—so desired. The General replied that "this is not my decision—it is yours." Nixon replied rather crisply that he would be glad to take responsibility for the decision, either way. But first, he said, the public, and the General himself, ought to have a chance to "hear my side of the story." He bluntly warned Eisenhower against listening to "some of those people around you who don't know a damn thing about it." And he concluded by giving the conqueror of Hitler a brief lecture about practical politics.

The longer there remained any doubt about whether or not he was to stay on the ticket, Nixon said, the more harm it would do, not only to himself but to the whole ticket. In a situation of this sort, a decision had to be made, and it had to be made quickly. And according to at least three people who should know, Nixon concluded with a bluntly worded admonition.[1] Nixon's words were: "General, a time comes in politics when you have to pee or get off the pot."

It was a remarkably bold and aggressive line for a young man under bitter attack to take. But it worked, as Nixon knew that it must—neither Eisenhower nor anyone else could possibly drop Nixon from the ticket without giving Nixon a chance to tell "his side of the story." There had been talk of putting Nixon on a nationwide television hookup before the conversation with Eisenhower, but the money was not to be found. After that conversation, it was found, and before the night ended.

Nixon's famous broadcast the next Tuesday night, September 23, was his most decisive political triumph—after that, he could never again be written off as a mere Throttlebottom. But it is still even to this day, in some ways, a millstone around Nixon's political neck. Those who dislike Nixon often explain their dislike by pointing to "that tear-jerking soap opera about the fund." And some of those who cannot explain

[1] *Despite the Vice-President's rather half-hearted* dementi, *as recorded in the interview in the appendix, I have confidence in the awed and vivid recollection of these witnesses.*

their dislike for Nixon except in terms of his jowls probably
have the fund speech tucked away somewhere in their subconscious.

To understand why Nixon made the kind of speech he
did, it is necessary to go back to Nixon's youth, to the way
he was brought up, to the boy who was father of the man.
To do so is a fascinating exercise, for you can find in Nixon's
background the genesis of much of the content of the famous
speech. But here, you say to yourself, was how that "respectable Republican cloth coat" was born. And here is the shame-
less hamminess of the "little cocker spaniel dog, Checkers."
And here is how Nixon learned the debating tricks which he
used to score points—some wholly specious—off the Democrats. And here, finally, are the origins of that high moral
tone—that "Goddam holier-than-thou attitude"—which infuriated the passionate partisans of Adlai Stevenson more
than anything else in the speech. To understand why Nixon
made the sort of speech he made, in short, you have to understand how Nixon had come to be the sort of man he was,
and that attempt at understanding will be made in another
chapter. Here we are concerned with the way Nixon reacts
to a crisis, to a danger threatening himself. And for that purpose, the reactions of General Eisenhower, who heard the
speech in an auditorium in Cleveland, are well worth recording.

In the manager's office of the auditorium, Eisenhower was
surrounded by his large entourage, including a number of
those who had urged that Nixon be dumped from the ticket.
In his hand the General had a block of paper and a pencil.
Before Nixon was halfway through his highly emotional performance, many of those around the General were weeping,
and the tears of those who had urged Nixon's withdrawal
were particularly conspicuous.

"Ike wasn't crying though," testifies one astute observer
who sat close to him and who was clever enough to watch the

General instead of the television screen. "He was tapping the pad with his pencil. Twice he jabbed the pencil right into the pad, the second time so hard the lead broke. Before that, I'd always liked and admired Ike, of course, but I'd often wondered how smart he really was. After that, I knew—— Ike got what Dick was getting at right away, while the others were weeping and carrying on."

The General jabbed his pencil into the pad the first time when Nixon said:

"I would suggest that under the circumstances both Mr. Sparkman and Mr. Stevenson should come before the American people as I have, and make a complete financial statement as to their financial history. And if they don't, it will be an admission that they have something to hide, and I think you will agree with me."

There were, after all, four national candidates, not three, and the fourth was General Dwight D. Eisenhower. Had the General "something to hide"? He did not, of course. But it would have been highly embarrassing for him to make a "complete financial statement," in part because the military rarely get into the habit of making charitable contributions, and in part because such a statement would have drawn unnecessary attention to the "Eisenhower ruling," under which the General was permitted to pay capital-gains taxes rather than income taxes on his fabulous earnings from his book.

The General jabbed so hard that he broke the lead off his pencil when Nixon said:

"I would do nothing that would harm the possibilities of Dwight Eisenhower to become President of the United States; and for that reason I am submitting to the Republican National Committee tonight, through this television broadcast, *the decision it is theirs to make*. Let them decide whether my position on the ticket will help or hurt; and I am going to ask you to help them decide. Wire and write the Republican National Committee whether you think I should stay or whether I should get off; and whatever *their* decision is, I will abide by it."

"The decision it is theirs to make." Not, in other words, Eisenhower's to make. Nixon knew that, with the strong support of party chairman Arthur Summerfield and of Senator Robert A. Taft, he had an easy majority on the national committee. He had that easy majority even before the famous speech and whatever Eisenhower's inclinations might be. This, then, was a delicate way of saying to Eisenhower, "It is not up to you to decide whether I get off or stay on."

Nixon's final words were: "And remember, folks, Eisenhower is a great man, believe me. He is a great man, and a vote for Eisenhower is a vote for what is good for America." This amounted to a firm promise that, if he remained on the ticket, Nixon would go down the line for the head of the ticket. But the things which caused the General to jab his pad with his pencil also added up to a promise—and a warning.

To understand Nixon's warning, it is necessary to go back to an episode which occurred before the broadcast. Shortly before Nixon was scheduled to go on the air, Thomas E. Dewey called his headquarters, using a pseudonym, and insisted on speaking to him. With the authority of the man who was chiefly responsible for Nixon's nomination, Dewey told Nixon that he had to report "regretfully" that most of the party leadership believed that he ought to withdraw as the vice-presidential candidate. Dewey was also, after all, principally responsible for Eisenhower's nomination, and, although he did not say so explicitly, the clear implication of what he said was that Eisenhower was among the party leaders who wanted Nixon out of the way.

Nixon's response to this invitation to commit political suicide was contained in the passages quoted above. Those passages were Nixon's way of saying that, if an attempt were made to force him off the ticket, he would fight back with everything he had—and that he had plenty to fight with. The warning, moreover, was aimed directly at General Eisenhower.

Whatever else one thinks of Nixon, it is difficult for anyone who admires courage not to be impressed by the downright breathtaking boldness he displayed at this moment when he could so easily have been destroyed. More was to follow. After the speech, Eisenhower sent a congratulatory message to Nixon, only part of which reached Nixon over the radio. The gist of the part Nixon heard was a request to Nixon to come immediately to Wheeling, West Virginia, Eisenhower's next campaign stop, to see the General and to help him "complete the formulation of my personal decision." "My personal decision," mind you, not "the decision it is theirs to make." The General had indeed "got what Dick was getting at."

From Cleveland, Republican chairman Summerfield and his public relations expert, Robert Humphreys, together called Nixon's Los Angeles headquarters to make what they thought would be the purely routine arrangements for Nixon's joining the General in Wheeling. They were in a jubilant and confident mood, for they already knew that the Nixon speech had been a political triumph. They finally got through to Murray Chotiner. The conversation which ensued went about as follows:

"Well, Murray, how are things out there?"

"Not so good."

"What in hell do you mean, not so good?"

"Dick just wrote out a telegram of resignation for the General."

"WHAT? My God, Murray, you tore it up, didn't you?"

"Yes, I tore it up, but I'm not so sure how long it's going to stay torn."

A horrified pause.

"Well, Dick's flying to Wheeling to see the General, isn't he?"

"No. We're flying tonight to Missoula." (Missoula, Montana, was Nixon's next scheduled speaking engagement.)

"WHAT? My God, Murray, you've got to persuade him to come to Wheeling."

"Arthur, we trust you. If you can give us your personal assurance, direct from the General, that Dick will stay on the ticket with the General's blessing, I think I can persuade him. I know I can't otherwise."

Eisenhower's request to Nixon to meet him in Wheeling to hear his decision represented precisely the summons to be judged which Nixon was determined at all costs to avoid. So again Nixon took an amazingly bold and aggressive line, and again it worked, as Nixon knew that it must. After the enormous political triumph of his telecast, Nixon was no little boy, to be summoned for a spanking or a reward. He held the whip hand, and he knew it, and the Eisenhower party knew it, too. At dawn the next day, Summerfield, after a frantic night in which he had finally managed to reach the General when his train stopped briefly on its way across Ohio to Wheeling, called Murray Chotiner. He had the General's absolute promise, Summerfield told Chotiner, that Nixon would be welcomed with all honor in Wheeling, with no ifs, ands, or buts about his remaining on the ticket. For Nixon the victory was complete and unconditional. And so he enplaned for Wheeling, and the rest is history—how the General welcomed him with "Dick, you're my boy," how Nixon cried on Knowland's shoulder, and all the rest of it.

It was, surely, an extraordinary performance. Here was a man of thirty-nine, with only six years in politics, with a sure, instinctive grasp of the political realities and a bold willingness to act on those realities. Nixon knew that, if he demanded that his side of the case be heard, it would be politically impossible to deny him that right. Nixon knew, even before the broadcast, that although Eisenhower and most of the men around him might want to dump him, as

Dewey implied, they would think long and hard if Nixon made it clear that he was willing to fight with everything he had. Finally, once he knew that his broadcast had been a political triumph, Nixon also knew that the mere hint that he might resign, even that he might fail to accede to Eisenhower's public request that he come to Wheeling, would be enough to ensure his own unconditional victory.

A very astute and probably largely instinctive judgment of General Eisenhower, both as a human being and as a newly fledged politician, was certainly a decisive factor in Nixon's course during the fund crisis. Eisenhower had been in politics only a few months at the time. A few weeks before, the Scripps-Howard papers had charged that he was "running like a dry creek." He completely lacked the confidence in his political judgment which he later developed, as a result of experience and his two landslide elections. He was almost wholly dependent on the advice of those around him. And Dewey was certainly telling the truth when he reported to Nixon that most of that advice was to dump Nixon. At a meeting of the large Eisenhower entourage only two or three hours before the broadcast, Summerfield was the only one of those present who spoke up strongly for keeping Nixon.

In these circumstances, to be meek, to be defensive, was to commit political suicide. If Nixon had for one moment seemed to offer his head on a platter to Eisenhower, those around Eisenhower would have made certain that the offer was accepted—and not very gratefully. Nixon, in short, as the story of the fund crisis clearly shows, early reached the "analytical conclusion" that the key to victory or to a defeat from which he could never recover lay with Eisenhower; and further, that the way to deal with Eisenhower was to be aggressive, and tough as nails.

With another man, there might have been grave risks involved in this conclusion. It is hard to imagine a Franklin Roosevelt, or a Harry Truman, accepting the lecture on poli-

tics, with its final admonition, which Nixon gave Eisenhower
in that telephone conversation. It is hard to imagine them
reacting as Eisenhower reacted to Nixon's veiled threat to resign, conveyed through Chotiner, or his refusal to come to
Wheeling except on his own terms. At some point, if the ticket
had been headed by a self-confident, experienced, professional politician, Nixon would have been slapped down and
slapped down hard. But the outcome suggests how remarkably accurate was Nixon's judgment of Eisenhower, both as
a human being and as a totally inexperienced politician.

The second episode in which Nixon faced a major political crisis, and which also involved a judgment on his part of
Eisenhower's character, is more quickly told. It cannot be
told so confidently, however, because there is one unan-
swered—and for the present, at least, unanswerable—question
involved. The question is this: Did President Eisenhower seriously wish to replace Nixon as his running mate in 1956?

The bare facts are as follows: In February 1956, Eisenhower asked Nixon to come to the White House for a chat.
He adopted a benign and fatherly tone. He had decided, he
said, to run again for the presidency and he would so an-
nounce shortly. Nixon should consider his own future very
seriously. No Vice-President in modern history, the President
pointed out, had succeeded a living President. Nixon had
held elective office throughout his career. Might it not be
better for him to get some administrative experience? He
could certainly have a Cabinet post—defense, for example,
was a most challenging job. Might that not be better than to
run again for the vice-presidency?

Nixon was noncommittal in his response. But privately he
was dismayed. If the President did not want to dump him as
his running mate, he had certainly sounded as though he
did. For a time Nixon seriously considered taking the lucra-
tive partnership in private practice which he had been offered, and this time his wife, Pat, who had extracted from

him in 1954 a promise to retire from politics, favored his getting out.

On February 29, as he had told Nixon he would, the President announced that he would run again. Immediately, "Will Nixon run?" replaced "Will Eisenhower run?" as the favorite topic of speculation in the press. On March 7, the President added to the speculation by saying that Nixon should "chart his own course." On April 26, Nixon took matters into his own hands. He asked to see the President, said that he had thought over carefully what the President had said at their previous meeting, reminded him of his press-conference statement, and said that he had decided to run again for the vice-presidency, if the President and the Republican convention approved. The President replied that he was delighted by Nixon's decision. Nixon promptly announced it at the White House to the hastily assembled members of the White House press corps, while Jim Hagerty (a consistent Nixon man in the Administration) bore emphatic witness to the President's "delight."

Was the President really delighted? Or had that first conversation been his way of suggesting politely to Nixon that he step aside? There are those who know both men who believe that Eisenhower was sincerely advising Nixon in what he regarded as Nixon's own best interest. That may be. It would suggest a quite remarkable political naïveté in the President, but then in some ways the President has always been remarkably naïve in matters political, where his own political popularity has not been involved. Other credible witnesses are sure that the President had in fact been persuaded by some of those around him that it would be wiser to replace Nixon, especially in view of his own recent heart attack, and that his February talk with Nixon was Eisenhower's gentle way of beginning the process of replacement.

This latter view is lent some credibility by the bizarre episode of Harold Stassen's futile attempt to dump Nixon as the

President's running mate and replace him with Christian A. Herter. Whatever one may think of Stassen, he is, after all, an experienced politician. It is hard to believe that even Stassen would launch his dump-Nixon movement without some real reason to believe that the move might succeed— and it could succeed only with at least the tacit backing of the President. Queried on this point, Stassen will say only that "the whole story cannot now be told," which hints strongly that Stassen *did* have some reason to believe that the President wished to replace Nixon.

However that may be, after that fatherly talk in February, Nixon himself had good reason to suppose that the President wanted another running mate. But it is obvious that again, as in the 1952 crisis, Nixon "considered all the worst alternatives and reached an analytical conclusion." He quickly concluded that if he were to accept the President's offer and step down into a Cabinet post, he would be finished politically. He also concluded—and this took a good deal more thought, no doubt, since he had that big offer from a California law firm and Pat had had her fill of politics—that he wanted to finish what he had begun. And finally he obviously also concluded that in 1956, as in 1952, the best course was an aggressive course. Hence his decision to seize the initiative. For once Nixon had announced his decision to run again from the White House itself, with Hagerty at his side to say with emphasis that the President was "delighted," there was no way on earth to force Nixon off the ticket, short of a public and unequivocal decision by the President himself to do the forcing.

Again there was a risk involved, as in 1952. Another kind of President (the names of Roosevelt and Truman come again to mind) might have resented Nixon's course as an attempt to force his hand. That kind of President might have told the Vice-President then and there that he wanted another running mate. But again Nixon correctly judged his man. And again he had plucked the flower of safety from the nettle of danger. In both crises the risk had been very great, and in both Nixon's triumph was unconditional.

Murray Chotiner, who admires Nixon as a politician much as a great modern art expert might admire Picasso as an artist, has said that Nixon has two qualities which distinguish him from lesser members of the political breed. He is "always willing to go for broke." And "he always moves fast to shape events."

Both qualities were displayed by Nixon on the two occasions when his political life was in danger. They were also displayed on the one occasion when his physical life was in danger.

Nixon's "good-will" tour of South America may have been a diplomatic misfortune but it was unquestionably for Nixon a political triumph. After the South American trip, Nixon's standing in the polls took a sudden leap, just as they did after his trip to the Soviet Union—and the polls may have a decisive influence on Nixon's future (and indeed on the future of the United States). If simple guts, plus an ability to think quickly and well in a moment of great physical danger, are admirable qualities, then Nixon's South American triumph was deserved.

The story of Nixon's South American tour has been told in detail elsewhere, especially in Earl Mazo's book, which is a remarkable job of detailed reporting. Here I shall confine myself to the incident which impressed me most when Nixon described the South American trip to me at some length, shortly after his return. The incident occurred in Caracas, Venezuela, which was Nixon's last stop on his South American tour, and which could quite well have been his last stop on earth.

As soon as he landed at the airport, Nixon knew that he and his party were in bad trouble—worse trouble than in Peru, where rocks had been thrown at him at San Marcos

University in Lima. The airport at Caracas was flooded with
a screaming mob of teen-agers out of control, led and egged
on by Communists. To get to their car, the Nixons had to
pass through "a rain of spit," as Nixon put it, but worse was
to come.

Nixon's first scheduled stop in Caracas was to be a traditional wreath-laying ceremony at Simón Bolívar's tomb in
Pantheon Plaza. All the way into town the Nixon motorcade
was harried and chevied by rock-throwing mobs, while the
Venezuelan police assigned to protect the Vice-President
faded away. Four blocks short of the Plaza the motorcade
came to a dead stop, halted by a roadblock of trucks on the
divided six-lane highway, and the mob closed in on the lead
car, in which Nixon was riding with the Foreign Minister.

Nixon's description of what followed has a bizarre Wal-
purgisnacht quality. He was riding in a Cadillac—Pat, just
behind him with the wife of the Foreign Minister, was also
in a Cadillac. The windows of both cars, which were rolled
up as protection against the mob, were covered with spit and
vegetable matter, through which the hate-filled faces of the
mob, pressed in close against the car on all sides, were
strangely distorted. The invention of shatterproof glass probably saved Nixon's life. He had not realized before, he says,
how hard it is to break a good car window. He remembers
one man beating at the glass with an iron pipe. Even when
the pipe finally broke the glass, most of the window remained
intact. A big rock, Nixon remembers, which had been hurled
at the car, was embedded in one of the windows and supported by the glass.

A mere handful of American Secret Service men were the
only protection for the Nixon party—aside from that invalu-
able shatterproof glass—and although they did yeoman service, they could not control a mob of thousands. When the mob
began to rock the car, Nixon realized fully for the first time
that his life, and his wife's, and the lives of the other people

in the party, were in real danger. South American mobs share with those of the Middle East an unpretty propensity for dismembering their victims in the streets—in the uprising against the Pérez Jiménez dictatorship, some months before, a number of unpopular persons had shared this unpleasant fate.

Nixon was not consciously frightened. When a crisis is going on, he says, "I feel cold, matter of fact, analytical," although afterward he may feel physically ill. But he knew that somehow his car and his wife's must escape from that place where they were seemingly trapped forever. And he therefore began to consider—coldly, matter of factly, and analytically—the height of the concrete island which ran down the middle of the big boulevard. There was no way to get through the roadblock in the right lane. But the left lane going the other way was quite empty. Could the Cadillacs clear the concrete island and thus escape?

The arrival of a handful of troops brought a small temporary clearing of the space immediately in front of the cars. Nixon says: "I made a command decision." Word was passed to the cars behind, and on orders from Nixon (the Foreign Minister had by this time been reduced to a state of incoherence) the big car started for the concrete island, bumped over it, and, followed by Mrs. Nixon's Cadillac, tore up the empty opposite lane the wrong way.

At this point Nixon says, "I made another command decision." He ordered the chauffeur to go directly to the American Embassy. The Foreign Minister, suddenly reviving, weakly protested that Nixon was expected next at the wreath-laying ceremony, but Nixon briskly overruled him. It was fortunate that he did so, because another, and larger, Communist-led mob was awaiting him at Bolívar's tomb, and this mob was armed, not only with rocks but also with explosives.

There is a great deal more, of course, to the story of Nixon in South America, but there is nothing that throws more light on Nixon's reaction to crisis than those two "command decisions." There is no doubt at all that Nixon's life was in danger. Reliable American reporters on the spot confirm that the danger was quite real, and so do intelligence estimates of the situation made after the event. Nixon—and perhaps others, including his wife—was saved, in part by the safety glass, in part by the intrepidity of Secret Service agents, but also in part by Nixon's "cold, matter of fact, analytical" response to crisis.

Nixon, in short, has guts. No sensible person, however hostile to Nixon in other ways, can deny him that quality. He has other qualities, some admirable, some not so admirable. But the quality of guts is the quality which mostly marks him.

"When somebody launches an attack, your instinct is to strike back," Nixon says. "If you're always on the defensive, you always lose in the end." These sentences suggest why the word "guts" is the correct word to describe the quality Nixon displayed in the three most dangerous crises of his career. For the word implies a certain aggressive toughness, a willingness to use means not necessarily laid down in the rule books, which such more elegant words as "courage" and "bravery" do not imply. The possession of guts obviously does not in itself qualify a man for the presidency. But in these times it is, nevertheless, a useful quality for a President to have.

5

The Two Rockefellers

Lame duck though he may be, if President Eisenhower wished to do so, he could make or break Nixon or Rockefeller. An incumbent President always has this power. Theodore Roosevelt had only to mention to a few intimates that he wanted William Howard Taft, and Taft—much to Roosevelt's later chagrin—it was. Harry Truman chose Adlai Stevenson in 1952, and Stevenson it would have been without further fuss, if Stevenson had not made the fuss. With his prestige and his presidential powers, Eisenhower could certainly have his way, if he decided to descend into the hurly-burly and fight for Rockefeller against Nixon, or vice versa.

But it seems a safe fifty-to-one bet that Eisenhower will not descend into the hurly-burly, that he will maintain a strict hands-off attitude until the last ballot is counted. The President dislikes the political hurly-burly in any case. But he also has a peculiar theory, which is certainly original with him (unless one goes right back to George Washington), that a President has no business trying to influence the choice of his party in convention assembled. It was in accordance with this odd theory that Eisenhower refused, right up to convention time in 1956, to endorse Nixon as his running mate, to the Vice-President's extreme annoyance.

The President, to be sure, has let it be known that there are limits to his private hands-off theory, as when he remarked in a 1959 press conference that he would intervene against any candidate who "opposed my policies." This gentle hint was almost certainly directed at Nixon, who had shown a tendency to stray off the Eisenhower reservation. In the early spring of 1958, for example, Nixon had come out semi-publicly in support of Secretary of Labor Mitchell's call for a tax cut to spur the economy, which was flatly contrary to Administration policy. But the issue on which Nixon came closest to alienating Eisenhower was the defense issue. Both in the pre-Sputnik and post-Sputnik eras, Nixon argued strongly within the Administration for a stepped-up defense program. During the heated defense debate in the early months of 1959, it was reported that Nixon privately agreed with critics of the Administration position.

There was no issue, as Nixon was certainly aware, on which Eisenhower felt more passionately. Nixon therefore called in a half-dozen key reporters and strongly defended the Eisenhower defense policy. This episode suggests that Nixon himself believed that a failure on his part to support the Administration defense policy might have bestirred the President to intervene against him in 1960.

In public and in private, to be sure, both Nixon and the President protest an undying devotion to each other. The real relationship can only be guessed at. No doubt the President does admire Nixon in some ways, notably for his guts and his political acumen. No doubt Nixon admires the President in other ways, and for other reasons. But the stubborn fact remains that Eisenhower seriously considered dumping his controversial running mate, both in 1952 and 1956. On both occasions Nixon "moved quickly to shape events"—and events were shaped as Nixon wanted them to be shaped, but not necessarily as the President wanted them to be shaped. The President is not a fool, as that memorable little scene when he broke his pencil lead in the Cleveland auditorium suggests. He would not be human if he had not felt some twinges of resentment against his aggressive subordinate. It can be reported on good authority that he has felt such twinges.

If the President were a passionate admirer of Rockefeller, those twinges might assume a profound historical significance. In fact, the evidence suggests that, while doubtless the President also admires Rockefeller in some ways, he is not really a passionate admirer of either man. He neither likes nor dislikes either enough to make a major effort to make or break either. This is another reason to suppose that Eisenhower will be neutral in spirit, as well as in deed, if a war to the knife develops between Nixon and Rockefeller.

It is no secret that Rockefeller did not greatly enjoy working for Eisenhower. Both as Under Secretary of Health, Education and Welfare in the first Eisenhower administration and as special cold-war adviser to the President, Rockefeller felt frustrated and unhappy a good deal of the time. Rockefeller's final frustration, which occurred in the second Eisenhower administration, has not, as of this writing, been previously described.

Early in 1957, Rockefeller was informed that, as a deserving Republican who had not been rewarded according to his deserts, he was to be offered the post of Deputy Secretary of Defense by the President. Although it was still a subordinate post, like his two previous jobs under Eisenhower, Rockefeller was delighted. Defense had long been one of his special interests; the job might well be a steppingstone to the Secretaryship of Defense; and in any case it offered Rockefeller just the kind of authority and responsibility he had theretofore lacked.

But then Secretary of the Treasury George Humphrey got wind of the intended appointment and immediately protested as strongly as he knew how—which is very strongly indeed—to the President. It would be a cardinal error, Humphrey maintained, to put a "spender" like Rockefeller in a key defense job. The President, always remarkably subject to Humphrey's influence, promptly reversed himself, and Rockefeller was told he was not to be made Deputy Defense Secretary after all.

There the episode ended. Rockefeller, as far as is known, has never said a word about it, in private or public. But it had its effect on Rockefeller. It finally persuaded him that there was only one way for a very rich man like himself to achieve what he had always wanted—real political power and authority. That way was to be elected to high office. Almost immediately after he had been turned down for the defense post, Rockefeller began the complicated process of study and analysis which always precedes any major Rockefeller decision. As a result, long before the end of 1957, and before there was even a whisper of a whisper of a Rockefeller boom, he had decided that he had at least an outside chance for the New York governorship, and he had further decided to make a try for it.

Had it not been for George Humphrey's intervention, Rockefeller would not be governor of New York today and Richard Nixon would have had clear sailing to the nomination. Thus it is at least possible—a lovely irony—that George Humphrey, in keeping a "spender" out of a subordinate Defense Department post, put that same "spender" into the White House.

By his own lights, of course, Humphrey was quite right

to intervene. Rockefeller has always given the national security a higher priority than a balanced budget or reduced
taxes, thus reversing the Humphrey system of priorities. The
kind of defense policy he would have favored is suggested by
the report on defense which he sponsored and largely paid
for, and which was published in January 1958. The report
proposed a sharp and continuous increase in defense spending in order to maintain a reasonable balance of power with
the Soviet bloc. If Rockefeller had been permitted to take the
defense post, the policy of maintaining a true power balance
would at least have had a strong advocate in the Administration. It is possible that, as a result, Khrushchev would not be
quite so cockily confident that the power balance has now
shifted heavily in his favor, as he constantly boasts. In any
case, the President's reversal on the Rockefeller appointment
marked the moment when he finally and fully embraced the
Humphrey order of priorities, about which he had previously
evinced some doubts.

The episode of Eisenhower's withdrawn offer to Rockefeller suggests an obvious conclusion. Eisenhower will not fight,
bleed, and die—nor will he lift a finger—to get the nomination
for Rockefeller. Why, after all, should he favor the presidential candidacy of a man who, he was persuaded, was unfitted
by his tendencies as a "spender" for a sub-Cabinet post? To
sum up, if Eisenhower does not greatly admire either Nixon
or Rockefeller, why should he intervene in favor of either of
them?

There is a sharp contrast between the records of Nixon and
Rockefeller in Eisenhower's Washington. From the fund crisis on, Nixon almost always got his way with Eisenhower. Not
quite always, to be sure. Early in the second Eisenhower administration, Nixon was eager to be appointed chairman of
the obscure but powerful Operations Coordination Board.
The OCB, which is supposed to follow through on decisions
of the National Security Council, has its fingers in every pie,

and the job would have provided Nixon with useful experience and contacts. The President vetoed the idea, however, much to Nixon's disappointment and annoyance, on the grounds that a Vice-President has no constitutional business holding a job in the executive branch. Nixon has also been occasionally disappointed and annoyed by the President's tendency to treat him as a politician, and nothing more—the President listens with respect to his views on politics, but tends to interrupt him and dismiss his opinions on other subjects.

But the fact remains that, by and large, Nixon has had his way in Eisenhower's Washington. Above all, he has been able to use the vice-presidential office as a steppingstone toward the presidency as no other Vice-President in history has been able to do. By contrast, Rockefeller's experience in Eisenhower's Washington was a long exercise in frustration. And the contrast is not only with Nixon. It is also with Rockefeller himself—the younger Rockefeller who came to Washington in 1940 to work for Franklin D. Roosevelt.

Let us have a look at that younger Rockefeller. In the ten years after he had graduated from Dartmouth in 1930, Nelson Rockefeller was a frenetically busy man, as he will be to the day he dies. But he was busy mostly at the business of being a Rockefeller.

His most important individual achievement was his marriage to Mary Todhunter Clark, of a distinguished Philadelphia family—it was thought among the old Philadelphia families at the time that Mary Clark had married beneath her station. Like Pat Nixon in Nixon's life, "Tod" Rockefeller is an important factor in Rockefeller's life, although in both cases the men decidedly wear the family pants. Mrs. Rockefeller is very tall—taller than Nelson—and she has an original mind, liberal political views (she was a member of New York's Liberal party until shortly before her husband ran for governor), and a sense of humor. The sense of humor is important, since Rockefeller, like most fiercely ambitious men (Nixon, for example), tends to an excessive earnestness about everything, and Mrs. Rockefeller thus acts as a much needed balance wheel in the family.

The newlyweds established themselves on the vast family estate near Tarrytown on the Hudson, and in six years, with Nelson Rockefeller's usual enthusiasm and desire to get things done, they produced five children. Meanwhile they traveled around the world and over much of South America, where Nelson interested himself in the great oil holdings of the Rockefeller-controlled Creole Corporation. Rockefeller also managed to keep himself busy in innumerable directorships and other odd jobs connected with the family interest: as a director and in 1938 president of Rockefeller Center, and as a trustee and in 1939 president of the Museum of Modern Art.

The Museum of Modern Art was, and is, one of the really big things in Rockefeller's life. When the museum caught fire some years ago, Rockefeller insisted on borrowing a fireman's uniform and rushing into the burning building, like a parent rescuing a beloved child. In fact, Rockefeller's interest in art is entirely genuine. If he ever goes to the White House, he will fill the old mansion to the eaves with Picassos, Mondrians, Matisses, Paul Klees, and the like (which will no doubt become an "issue" like Harry Truman's balcony). Unlike many other rich men, he is not the kind of art collector who buys pictures as investments, like hog futures. He really loves pictures. Indeed, he is an aesthete, in the dictionary meaning of the word—"one very sensitive to the beauties of art or nature." Yet even the museum, like Rockefeller Center or Creole Petroleum or the other things that kept him busy in those days, was a family project rather than something he did on his own, as an individual rather than as a Rockefeller. The museum had been founded by his mother, Abby Aldrich

Rockefeller, and as one of her pet projects had been largely financed by her.

And yet Rockefeller's beloved museum gave him his first chance to do something important on his own, not as a Rockefeller but as Nelson Rockefeller. After he became president of the museum, Rockefeller planned a radio show, on a national hookup, celebrating its splendors. With typical self-confidence, he decided to get the President of the United States to star in his show. Franklin Roosevelt had no more interest in modern art than Harry Truman and Dwight D. Eisenhower (which is none at all). But he welcomed an opportunity, in those days of the Nazi threat to all civilized values, to make a speech about culture. And so Nelson Rockefeller met the President and thus got his first chance to branch out on his own.

The two got on well right away. Roosevelt always had something of a penchant for millionaires (Averell Harriman and Vincent Astor are examples). Moreover, although the Rockefellers were loyal Republicans, they were by no means the kind of Republicans, then very prevalent among the rich and their toadies, who turned puce-faced and incoherent at the mention of Roosevelt's name. "I'm increasingly bored by hearing attacks on the Roosevelts," Abby Aldrich Rockefeller, Nelson's mother, had written in 1935 when the hate-Roosevelt movement first began to gather steam, "and depressed by the bad taste that prompts them." Perhaps the President was aware of this Rockefeller tendency, which was wildly eccentric among the rich in those days, to regard him as less than the devil incarnate—and with war on the horizon, he doubtless saw advantages in having a representative of the biggest capitalist family in his Administration. At any rate, the President took a shine to the young man.

When the two met before the radio show, Rockefeller seized the opportunity to talk about a subject which he knew at firsthand, and which was already something of a King

Charles Head with him—Axis infiltration and propaganda in South America. The President expressed a casual desire to hear more. Rockefeller wrote a memorandum on the subject and got it to the President through Harry Hopkins, who had also taken a shine to him. The upshot was the creation, in August 1940, of the Office of the Coordinator of Inter-American Affairs, with young Nelson Rockefeller, at thirty-two, in the exalted post of coordinator.

The Rockefeller agency rather rapidly grew to around five thousand government workers—a respectable number for those days. With his own big agency, and with direct access to the President, Rockefeller was a far bigger mover and shaker on the Washington scene than he was ever to be again.

Most witnesses—though by no means all—of his performance in his role as coordinator, and later in the role of Assistant Secretary of State for South American Affairs, agree that he performed usefully as a wartime bureaucrat. Some go further and say that his operations in South America were brilliantly successful and should have set the pattern for all future American dealings with the underdeveloped countries. There is no doubt at all that Rockefeller is still genuinely popular in South America even today—the Communists could hardly have organized against him the kind of mass demonstrations they stage-managed against Nixon.

But all witnesses, critics and admirers, agree on one point. In the fierce and bloody battles which took place continually within the richly proliferating wartime bureaucracy, the fledgling Rockefeller held his own remarkably well. He defended his own empire with a single-minded ferocity, and he was not at all averse to carving a slice or two out of someone else's empire. In the process he made enemies, for the first time in his young life. That was inevitable, of course. What is interesting is how he made his enemies, and why. In this respect, a few episodes are revealing.

There was, for example, the matter of his falling out with

Carl Spaeth. Spaeth, now dean of Stanford Law School, was
in those days one of Rockefeller's closest friends, perhaps the
closest friend he had. He had graduated from Dartmouth the
year before Rockefeller—a high proportion of Rockefeller's associates are Dartmouth men—and he had worked with Rockefeller on various projects in South America before the war.
Rockefeller brought him to Washington as his deputy and
installed the Spaeths in his Washington home. For a time the
two men were the Damon and Pythias of the Washington
scene.

Then something happened. Spaeth left the Rockefeller
agency, and he and his wife left the Rockefeller house—
abruptly, according to one report, and with Mrs. Spaeth in
tears. Rockefeller and Spaeth wholly ceased to play Damon
and Pythias. Spaeth got a job with the South American di-
vision of the State Department. In 1944, when his agency
was being liquidated, Rockefeller was offered the post of Assistant Secretary of State for South American Affairs. He
accepted on one condition—that Spaeth find "other employment." His condition was, in short, that Spaeth be fired.

The trouble between the two men began, apparently, when
Spaeth, an ambitious man who likes to have his own way,
started making decisions on his own, without consulting
Rockefeller (Rockefeller has remarked that as a result of this
experience he will never again have a single "deputy" whose
title and position imply the right to move independently).
The trouble got worse when Rockefeller discovered, or was
led to believe, that Spaeth was attempting to carve out a separate bureaucratic empire for himself in South America, at the
expense of both Henry Wallace's Board of Economic War-
fare and Rockefeller's agency. And the break became final
when Spaeth, working with a committee of South Americans,
proposed that his committee have the power to counteract
Axis propaganda in South America. This proposal Rockefeller

interpreted as an attempt to undercut his agency's propaganda function in South America.

But the details of this ancient bureaucratic battle between former friends are unimportant. All passion is now spent, and Spaeth and Rockefeller are again on speaking terms. What is interesting about the episode is that it suggests that Rockefeller is decidedly jealous of his power and prerogatives (as, it may be worth noting, all strong Presidents have been). It also suggests the degree of personal allegiance which Rockefeller expects from those around him.

"Nelson doesn't expect you to be a yes-man," one of his associates has said. "But he does expect you to be a Rockefeller man, first, last, and all the time." The men around Rockefeller today are just that—Rockefeller men first, last, and all the time. If Rockefeller ever does move to the White House, whether in 1961 or 1965, every man and woman around him will have a similar allegiance.

Other episodes of Rockefeller's wartime days cast a revealing light on the kind of man he is, the kind of politician he has become, and the kind of President he might be. He is a man who wants—indeed, who passionately wants—to have his own way, and who is willing to fight for it, so long as there is a chance of victory. Take, for example, the policy dispute over the admission of Argentina to the United Nations. Almost everybody has forgotten now about this ancient battle, but it was a furious one at the time. Even today, Rockefeller and those who were involved in the dispute on both sides still have passionate views on the issue—Rockefeller is capable of going on at quite inordinate length on the subject.

Argentina had played footsie with the Axis during the war, although after the Act of Chapultepec a belated and purely *pro forma* Argentinian declaration of war against the Axis had been issued. The Soviets were loudly opposed to Argentina's admission into the United Nations. Soviet opposition was, of course, strictly cynical and wholly for bargaining purposes—at one point the Soviets hinted privately that they would not object to Argentina if the United States would support recognition of Poland's Lublin government. But there were also respectable moral reasons for casting Argentina into outer darkness—there had been some sporadic and rather languid official anti-Semitism in the country, for example, in pale imitation of the Nazis. Secretary of State Cordell Hull, with the support of such top State Department officials as Dean Acheson, James Dunn, and Spruille Braden, wanted to give Argentina its comeuppance and strongly opposed any invitation to Argentina to join the U.N.

Rockefeller, on the other hand, passionately believed that the only practical policy was to make peace with Argentina —otherwise, he argued, what seemed to be an American effort to discipline one South American nation would be bitterly resented by all South American nations. Feelings ran high —very high indeed. A participant recalls one heated top-level State Department meeting at which James Dunn flatly accused Rockefeller of misrepresenting official American policy toward Argentina in cables marked NOT FOR DISTRIBUTION. With considerable drama Dunn produced the cables which, he claimed, proved his point, and there was an unholy row.

There were other unholy rows. At the San Francisco Conference there was a fierce dispute within the American delegation, both about admission of Argentina and about a related issue, Article Fifty-one. Article Fifty-one laid down the principle that a group of states could band together to repel aggression. This was in accordance with the Act of Chapultepec, which Rockefeller had chiefly engineered, and which Argentina had accepted, thereafter declaring war on the Axis. Rockefeller, of course, was passionately in favor of Article Fifty-one, which the Soviets opposed.

He therefore invited Senator Arthur Vandenberg, chief Republican foreign-policy spokesman at the time, to dine with him in his suite in the St. Francis Hotel and laid his case before him. Vandenberg then passed the word that he would resign from the American delegation if the delegation did not insist on Article Fifty-one. Other members of the delegation were infuriated by Rockefeller's move, not least Vandenberg's fellow Republican, John Foster Dulles. In an angry scene, Dulles accused Rockefeller of ruining patient weeks of effort to hold Vandenberg in line.

When Rockefeller had his way, and Argentina was admitted and Article Fifty-one included in the Charter, the feelings of those he had defeated were by no means tender toward him. After Hull was out of office, Rockefeller made several efforts to see him so that he could make his peace with the old man (this, too, is typical of Rockefeller, for although he is willing to make enemies, he does not like to have unnecessary enemies). All his efforts were unavailing. Finally he approached Thomas Blake, then a State Department official, who was close to Hull for family reasons. He asked Blake to telephone Hull and ask for an appointment for him. Blake knew what Hull's reaction would be, but he obligingly called him and then held out the receiver toward Rockefeller. The old man's bellow was embarrassingly audible: "YOU CAN TELL THE YOUNG WHIPPERSNAPPER TO GO TO HELL." Rockefeller smiled rather pallidly, turned on his heel, and left Blake's office without another word.

When James Byrnes replaced Edward Stettinius as Secretary of State, the bureaucratic wheel came full circle. Byrnes asked Dean Acheson to be his Under Secretary, and Acheson agreed on condition that Rockefeller find "other employment." Acheson, in other words, demanded that Rockefeller be fired, just as Rockefeller had demanded that Spaeth be fired. The final episode of this era of Rockefeller's government service is also worth telling.

After Byrnes replaced Stettinius, Rockefeller found himself in purdah. Every attempt to see the new Secretary of State was met with a run-around. Finally, Rockefeller bulled his

way into Byrnes's office to tell him that he planned to give
a very important speech in Boston on policy toward Argentina and that he wished to confer with Byrnes first. Byrnes,
who had agreed to Acheson's condition, listened courteously
and then said gently: "Well, Nelson, I don't think we ought
to worry about that now. The President has decided to accept your resignation."

Rockefeller gulped, for he was, of course, quite smart
enough to know when he was being fired. He told Byrnes
he felt very strongly about the matters he wished to discuss
in the Boston speech and hoped he could make the speech
as his last act as an Assistant Secretary of State. Byrnes allowed as how it might be better all round if he resigned immediately. At this point, no doubt, that "curious narrowing
of the eyes" occurred. Rockefeller told Byrnes that, if he were
not permitted to make the speech as Assistant Secretary, he
would make it as Nelson Rockefeller and he would "tell the
whole story" of how South American policy has been idioti-
cally mishandled over his protests. He made the speech as
Assistant Secretary of State.

Immediately thereafter he "resigned." Spruille Braden, his
fiercest policy opponent, took his place. And to complete the
circle (and also, one suspects, as a slap at the departed Rockefeller) Carl Spaeth was brought back as Braden's special assistant.

In retrospect, Rockefeller seems to have been right in his
basic positions—Spruille Braden's subsequent experiment in
getting tough with the Argentinians was hardly an unquali-
fied success. But that is not the main point. For our purposes
the main point is that on the basic issues Rockefeller had his
way—and he had his way, as a young and comparatively junior official, against the combined opposition of some of the
most powerful men in Washington, including, on some issues, all three of the Secretaries of State under whom he
served. In the kind of battles in which he fought, moreover,

his money was no asset. Indeed, rather the opposite—there is an automatic tendency to dismiss a man very rich by inheritance, and especially a very young, very rich man, as something of a fool. Altogether, it was a quite remarkable performance. The contrast provided by his second major appearance on the Washington scene, as an official in the Eisenhower administration, is really very odd and interesting.

In the years between 1945, when he was fired by Jimmy Byrnes, and 1953, when he was hired again by Eisenhower, Rockefeller briefly held an advisory post with Truman's Point Four program. But his chief interest in those years was the International Basic Economy Corporation, or IBEC. IBEC oddly combined the ingrained Rockefeller habits of both making money and also handing it about. IBEC was, and is, concentrated largely in South America, Rockefeller's old stamping ground, and its policy is based on the ancient precept: "The Lord helps them who help themselves." The idea was that capital investment in a whole series of projects, from sewage-disposal plants to modern dairies, would improve the standard of life in the countries where the investment was made and, incidentally in the long run, make money for Rockefeller.[1]

In the early period after Rockefeller started IBEC, the eleemosynary aspects of the venture tended to overshadow the more practical considerations. In fact, IBEC lost a great deal of money to begin with. His friend Thomas Braden has quoted Rockefeller on what happened: "I had to go to Father because the company had to have a million dollars.[2] Father looked at the balance sheet and told me he would lend it to

[1] *Rockefeller laid down one firm rule, however—not a penny of investment in oil.*

[2] *That Rockefeller had to go to his father for so comparatively paltry a sum as a million dollars suggests the extent to which the Rockefeller fortune, as noted in Chapter 2, is frozen.*

me on one condition: that I use the money to liquidate the
company. I said 'Very well, Father,' and I went out and I
raised a million dollars on my own."

IBEC is now reported safely in the black. But although
IBEC interested Rockefeller and kept him busy, his heart
really still belonged to Washington and government service.
The Rockefellers backed Dwight D. Eisenhower against
Robert A. Taft for the nomination in 1952 and contributed
handsomely to the Eisenhower war chest. In 1953, accord-
ingly, Rockefeller was offered the post of Under Secretary of
the Department of Health, Education and Welfare. It was
hardly a large, ripe, and juicy plum. The Department, newly
created by Eisenhower, was the lowest in the departmental
pecking order, and the Secretary, and thus Nelson's boss, was
a woman, Oveta Culp Hobby. But Rockefeller took the job
with seeming enthusiasm. Indeed, the enthusiasm may have
been real. Already, the idea of going into elective politics had
entered his mind—as early as 1950 he discussed with friends,
not altogether idly, the notion of running for mayor of New
York or even for governor. It may have seemed to him that
experience in a purely domestic area of government might
be useful—as indeed it has been.

But where was the fierce infighter and bureaucratic empire builder of other days? In this second Washington appearance the face which Rockefeller turned to the world was
the face of a genial, enthusiastic, but not very effective "Indian"—as the second-level bureaucrats without real power
are known nowadays in Washington.[3] A senator describes the
impression Rockefeller made on those who saw him in action:

[3] *The word spread from the Pentagon, the "Chiefs" being the
Joint Chiefs of Staff and the "Indians" being the lower-ranking officers
who crowd around them at meetings with the other Chiefs to make
certain that they don't give an inch in the ancient battle between the
services.*

"Oveta would always take Rockefeller to all the hearings, but she did all the talking. Sometimes she'd say, 'Now Mr. Rockefeller will show you what I mean,' and Rockefeller would take a pointer and point something out on a chart, while Oveta went on talking. Any clerk could have done the job, but he seemed to enjoy it—always had a big smile."

A friend of Rockefeller's, who knew the inside workings of HEW and who was shown this senatorial quotation and asked to comment on it, wrote as follows:

"Every idea that came out of HEW was Nelson's. He plotted the organization that turned a lot of bureaus into an agency. He got the people together to work out the new social-security legislation and health reinsurance. He recruited all the new talent. In fact he ran the outfit. Now, if you're running the outfit from the number-two spot, you try very hard when in public to behave like a good number two. You don't try to overshadow your boss. And if your boss is a woman, and you're at a public hearing, you do the chart lifting, not she. Particularly when they're your charts, and it was your idea to put everything on charts, as Nelson always does."

All true, no doubt, though Mrs. Hobby might not agree in every detail. But the fact remains that the face Rockefeller turned to the world while he was working for Mrs. Hobby was the face of a dutiful and eager subordinate—which was, for Rockefeller, an entirely new face. He wore a similar public face in his second Eisenhower job, as a special adviser to the President, a post to which he was appointed in 1954. His duties were exceedingly ill-defined—the position derived from the chairmanship of a committee set up in the Truman era to try to make some sense out of American propaganda policy. Rockefeller's job was usually described as "advising the President on how to win the cold war."

It was a frustrating job. Among the chief frustrators were the powerful members of the "Four H Club"—Treasury Secretary Humphrey, Budget Director Hughes, foreign-aid chief

Hollister, and Under Secretary of State Hoover. Rockefeller's advice to the President on "how to win the cold war" usually involved spending money—Rockefeller argued, for example, for an expanded and more imaginative foreign-aid program. Rockefeller lost all such arguments hands down, thanks partly to the fact that the Four H Club had successfully pinned the label "spender" on him in the President's mind.

But the greatest frustrator of all was Secretary of State John Foster Dulles. As we have seen, Dulles's first official contact with Rockefeller, at the San Francisco U.N. Conference, was not exactly happy. Later, when the two happened to be seated next to each other at a dinner honoring Winston Churchill at the time of the famous Fulton speech, Dulles was magnanimous, in a mellow and avuncular way. He told Rockefeller that Rockefeller had been right, and he had been wrong, at San Francisco. If Rockefeller and Vandenberg had not insisted on the right of collective self-defense, as laid down in Article Fifty-one, Dulles said, the Soviets would have been in a far better position to pick off the free-world nations one by one.

At first, when Rockefeller became the President's special foreign-affairs adviser (a job Dulles had once rather fancied for himself) Dulles's attitude toward Rockefeller continued mellow and avuncular. But when Rockefeller began putting forward foreign-policy ideas of his own, the relationship quickly cooled. A participant at one meeting between Dulles and the President shortly before the 1955 summit conference recalls that the President mentioned the aerial inspection, or "open skies" plan, and that at first Dulles sounded rather sympathetic to the plan, saying something to the effect that it was well worth studying. The President then remarked that Nelson Rockefeller had first proposed it to him, and Dulles, with his brilliant lawyer's mind, immediately enumerated a long list of cogent reasons for rejecting the plan.

A participant at another pre-Geneva White House meeting recalls a somewhat similar episode. Dulles took the line that the essential purpose of the summit meeting would be simply to define the areas of disagreement, so that the foreign ministers could thereafter attempt to negotiate accommodations in those areas. At this point Rockefeller burst in to protest against so sterile an approach. He reminded the President of a public-opinion poll which he had had taken in various European countries, which showed that most Europeans considered the United States and the Soviet Union about equal threats to the peace. Here was an opportunity, Rockefeller said, to re-emphasize America's dedication to peace and to re-assert American leadership of the West.

Dulles then broke in to say that "we don't want to make this meeting a propaganda battlefield." The subject was changed by the President and the discussion continued for a time along the lines laid down by Dulles, when Rockefeller, unable to contain himself, again passionately protested that it would be fatal to give the Soviets the propaganda initiative on the peace issue. At this point the President testily interrupted Rockefeller to say, "Damn it, Nelson, I've already told you we don't want to make this meeting a propaganda battlefield."

As this suggests, in those days the voice of Dulles was quite literally the President's voice in matters concerning foreign policy. And although these two episodes also suggest that Rockefeller did not lose all his battles, Dulles used his great power with the President to frustrate most of Rockefeller's bright ideas for winning the cold war. In retrospect, Rockefeller does not blame Dulles—he has told friends that, since there can be only one Secretary of State, in Dulles's shoes he would no doubt have behaved as Dulles did. But it was an unhappy time for Rockefeller all the same. It was the time when he got his reputation, which is an article of faith in certain conservative Republican circles, as a "spender," a "boy scout," a "rich do-gooder," and a New Dealer in disguise.

His chief enemies and critics were the more right-wing Republicans in the Administration. But a good many of the upper-level civil servants who knew Rockefeller in his days as cold-war adviser also have a tepid opinion of him, at least in his capacity as a fellow bureaucrat. Rockefeller had a habit of summoning large numbers of government people to meetings, often at Quantico, which is inconveniently distant from Washington, and often over weekends, when civil servants (who in the higher bureaucratic echelons work a good deal harder than their opposite number in business) like to get a little rest. This may help to explain the rather sour view of Rockefeller held by a number of government officials, which was expressed by one of them as follows:

"You know what you have to do if you want to win on a big issue like foreign aid. You go to the press. You go to the key men on the Hill. You get access to the White House, one way or another. And you fight like hell. But Nelson did none of these things. He just called meetings, and you know how much meetings mean in Washington."

The reputation Rockefeller got in his second Washington appearance was, in short, in total contrast to his earlier reputation as an ambitious and ruthless infighter and empire builder. How explain the difference?

Part of the answer lies, of course, in the difference between Rockefeller's situation in the wartime forties and his situation in the Eisenhower fifties. As head of a big wartime agency Rockefeller possessed the sinews of bureaucratic power, which he largely lacked in the fifties.

Far more important, however, was the difference in his relationship with the President. Nowadays, Rockefeller's relationship with Franklin D. Roosevelt is no doubt a delicate subject. But the evidence suggests that Roosevelt had a profound influence on Rockefeller. Rockefeller not only liked and admired the President who gave him his first chance to prove himself on his own, he has also, one suspects, deliberately in some ways patterned himself on Roosevelt, just as Roosevelt deliberately patterned himself on his cousin Theodore. In any case, there are many ways in which Rockefeller is like his fellow member of the Hudson River squirearchy, from his peculiar methods of dealing with subordinates to the aura of confidence and optimism with which he surrounds himself. And there is no doubt that Rockefeller's relationship with Roosevelt was quite different from his relationship with Eisenhower.

Rockefeller was never in the Roosevelt Inner Circle, of course, but he was close enough to the wartime President so that he could always, in a pinch, appeal to the White House, which is a decisive weapon in the endless internecine wars in Washington. One former official in Rockefeller's wartime agency recalls his first day on the job, when a meeting was held to consider some long-forgotten policy dispute between the agency and the State Department. Rockefeller, after listening for a while, turned casually to a secretary and said, "Get me the President." In a matter of minutes the new official faintly heard, to his amazement, the familiar voice, slightly mocking, slightly avuncular, over the telephone: "Well, Nelson, what is it now?"

There was no such relationship between Rockefeller and President Eisenhower. Rockefeller tried very hard, to be sure, to establish close personal relations with Eisenhower. He even had a one-hole golf course built on his Washington estate in the hope—or so all his acquaintances assumed—that the President would use the course for practice. But the hope was dashed—Eisenhower never so much as swung a club on the Rockefeller tee, while the self-made big businessmen who had the President's instinctive respect dismissed "young Rockefeller" as a "boy scout" or "do-gooder." A government official without real influence at the White House is pretty well licked before he starts, in any really major bureaucratic battle, and Rockefeller no doubt recognized that this was so.

Then there was also another reason why the tough empire builder of the Roosevelt days became the obedient Indian of the Eisenhower era. In the wartime days he simply wanted to have his way, on issues very close to his heart, and he did not very much care if he made a few important enemies in the process. In the fifties he was certainly thinking about his future, within the Administration and within the party. He doubtless hoped for just the kind of really important job he thought he was going to have in 1957, before George Humphrey intervened and snatched the prize away from him. He could not even hope for such a job if he got the reputation of "not playing with the team." And in a larger sense, since he was also beginning to think seriously of elective office, he did not want to alienate large numbers of important Republicans, notably including President Eisenhower himself.

But there is a final reason why Rockefeller got two such contrasting reputations in his two periods of service in Washington. There really is a lot of the boy scout or do-gooder in Rockefeller, just as there is a lot of the tough infighter and ambitious empire builder. To understand why this is so, it is necessary to understand something of Rockefeller's inheritance, which is unique, and also something about the environment in which he was brought up, which was also unique.

6

How They Got That Way: Rockefeller

At first blush it is difficult to imagine a contrast more complete than that provided by the circumstances to which Nelson Rockefeller and Richard Nixon were born.

On the one hand, the vast estates, centering on the great family fief on the Hudson River, the armies of servants, the famous and much hated name, and all about the invisible but almost tangible atmosphere of enormous wealth. On the other hand, the small frame house, the corner grocery store and gas station in a new California town, the daily chores, the hand-me-down clothes, the grinding worry about paying the doctors' bills.

And yet the contrast between the two families is not really

total after all. For there are certain striking similarities as
well. For example, both the Nixon and Rockefeller families
have a habit of remaining on earth for a good long time.
It was the ambition of Nelson Rockefeller's grandfather, the
first John D., to live to be a hundred, and he almost made it
—he was ninety-eight when he died in 1937. One of Nixon's
ancestors did make it—he lived to a fabulous 105—and both
Nixon's grandmother and his great-grandmother lived to
their mid-nineties.

There are more meaningful similarities. Nixon's grandmother and Rockefeller's grandmother were both, for example, founding members of the Women's Christian Tem-
perance Union. (Could they, perhaps, have known each
other? Both then lived in the Midwest, and the founding
members of the WCTU were a rather select band of ladies.)
Both families were active participants in the underground-
railway movement, bootlegging slaves into free territory before the Civil War. In both families racial tolerance is a
genuine tradition.

"There's the Quaker tradition of tolerance," Nixon says.
"We used to have Negroes and Mexicans working for us
sometimes, and we always ate at the same table—never
thought of anything else. A Quaker custom." Nelson Rockefeller's mother wrote to him and his brothers: "I want to make
an appeal to your sense of fair play and to beseech you to
begin your lives as young men by giving the other fellow, be
he Jew or Negro or of whatever race, a fair chance and a
square deal."

But the most obvious of the curious similarities in the backgrounds of these two men, superficially so dissimilar, is the
piety of their upbringing. The Nixon family routine called for
daily prayers and church four times on Sunday. The Rockefeller family routine was just as churchly, if not more so.

Both Nixon and Rockefeller, in fact, were brought up in an

atmosphere of family piety which was unique among the very rich when Rockefeller was a boy, already rare among the respectable poor when Nixon was a boy, and which has now almost wholly disappeared from the face of the earth, or at least from the face of the United States. Although the Nixon family was Quaker and the Rockefeller family Baptist, both were brought up to believe essentially the same things, notably that "life is real and life is earnest, and the grave is not its goal." This atmosphere of family piety and moral striving, which both men shared as boys, is at least as important to an understanding of them as the fact that Rockefeller was born very rich and Nixon was born respectably poor.

In Rockefeller's case, his grandfather, the first John D., was principally responsible for the family piety, as he was for so much else about the Rockefeller family. Old John D., who lived until Nelson was approaching thirty, and who was the unquestioned family patriarch and giver of laws until the moment of his death (and even in many ways thereafter), insisted on prayers before breakfast, permitted no liquor in his house, and aside from business reports read little but the Bible and the *Baptist Messenger*. His wife, Laura Spelman Rockefeller (she of the WCTU), was, if anything, even more pious. They brought up their only son, John D. Rockefeller, Jr. (known all his adult life as "Mr. Junior"), in a manner so rigidly prim that nowadays it would invite the attentions of the Child Welfare Society.

The Rockefellers were passionate prohibitionists. The first literature Mr. Junior got to heart was *The Price of a Drink:*

> *Five cents a glass, does anyone think*
> *That that is really the price of a drink? . . .*
> *The price of a drink, let him decide*
> *Who has lost his courage and his pride,*
> *And who lies a grovelling piece of clay,*
> *Not far removed from a beast today.*

"Our social life, looking back on it," Mr. Junior mildly re-marked to his biographer, Raymond Fosdick, "was cramped.
. . . Everything centered around the home and the church and there was nothing else." "My mother and father," Mr. Junior recalled at another time, "raised but one question: Is it right, is it duty?"

The haters of the first John D. wrote down this high moral outlook as the sheerest hypocrisy. And indeed the old man precisely fitted the stereotype of the top-hatted capitalist ruthlessly crushing widows and orphans on weekdays and acting the part of the pious churchman on Sunday. And yet the old man was no hypocrite. Hypocrisy is by definition a conscious state, for a man cannot pretend to be what he is not without knowing that he is pretending. And there was no pretending in old John D.'s piety.

He really never did see any contradiction between religion and his methods of making money. Indeed, since to him charity was an essential part of religion, the two went to-gether. "Make all you can, and give all you can," was his rule. Even when, as the son of an erratic peddler of quack cancer cures, he was still a struggling clerk, he gave strictly according to the Biblical injunction of the tithe. You can get an accurate guide to what his income was in any one year by multiplying his charities, of which he kept a meticulous record from his teens on, by ten. In 1885, for example, he was just moving into the really big time, for he gave away a quar-ter of a million, which meant an income of two and a half million. And by 1892 his income must already have been a fantastic (and gloriously tax-free) thirteen million, for his gifts that year came to a handsome $1,350,000.

In his own eyes the first John D.'s high moral outlook was entirely real, and he passed on to his descendants the same Baptist evangelism, the same moral idealism, in modern dress. To be sure, the upbringing of the third generation was less stifling than poor Mr. Junior's had been. But there were still prayers every morning, liquor and tobacco were still sternly discouraged, and that "one question"—is it right, is it duty?—was still asked. Today Nelson Rockefeller takes a glass of wine only as a social gesture, and whether he is talking domestic politics or foreign policy, a certain moral fervor marks his tone.

This annoys the cynics and infuriates those who disagree with him, causing them to dismiss him as a "boy scout" or a "damned do-gooder." But the moral fervor, like his grandfather's in a different context, is entirely real and very much part of the man. The fact is that, by certain cynical standards, Rockefeller *is* a do-gooder, both by inheritance and training.

But the moral outlook was not by any means all Nelson Rockefeller inherited from his father's side of the family. He also inherited, of course, a lot of money. Inheriting vast sums of money, as already noted, leaves its mark on any man. But this is true in a special sense in the case of a Rockefeller, for the Rockefeller name was hated more than that of any of the great robber-baron families. There was even a time when the first John D. had trouble giving away his money—"tainted money" it was called by respectable churchmen. And the effect of owning this kind of money is suggested by the terrible advice which Frederick T. Gates, a chief Rockefeller financial adviser, gave the unfortunate Mr. Junior when he was a young man: "In this business you have to live the life of a recluse. Never make friends. Don't join clubs. Avoid knowing people intimately."

Times have changed since that bleak advice was given, and so has the Rockefeller reputation. But even today, although Rockefeller has hosts of friendly acquaintances, he has few real intimates, as we have seen, and those he has are "Rockefeller men." Despite the hearty exuberance, there is also a guarded quality about the man—that "sudden curious narrowing of the eyes." This quality Nelson also shares with his

grandfather Rockefeller, whose rule it was to "expose as little
of the surface as possible."

There are other ways as well in which the influence of the
amazing old man still reaches strongly out from beyond the
grave. And the first John D., whatever else he was, *was* an
amazing man. He was a biological sport, a genius of sorts.
There is a fascination about the man, even to those who most
deplore him. Ida Tarbell, for example, one of the first of the
muckrakers and a very great reporter, who first exposed the
ruthless methods by which Standard Oil achieved its oil
monopoly, clearly had a sort of love-hate complex toward
her subject. She writes of "the legitimate greatness of Standard," by which she really meant, as the context makes obvious, the legitimate greatness of John D. Rockefeller.

As an economics major in college, Nelson Rockefeller read
Ida Tarbell's history of Standard Oil, and he thereafter remarked to a classmate: "My grandfather never broke a law,
but a lot of laws were passed because of him." This sums up
the old man's career about as well as it can be done in a sentence. But it does not reflect Nelson Rockefeller's genuine
affection for the totally bald, totally imperturbable old man
he knew when he was in his twenties and John D. was in his
nineties. Nelson Rockefeller was the old man's favorite grandson, and the two used to talk together often. The old man
certainly has a prominent place in Nelson's private pantheon
—no doubt incongruously close to Franklin D. Roosevelt.

Nelson remembers with affection his grandfather's large
collection of simple, old-fashioned jokes, always with a surprise ending. He remembers that, unlike most old men, his
grandfather only talked about the past if urged to do so—
he was chiefly interested in the present and future, and he
was rational and lucid on both subjects until the very end.
But what Nelson Rockefeller remembers best about his grandfather is a "sort of untouched quality," an ability to react to a

situation or a set of facts without being affected in the slightest by emotion.

In trying to describe this quality, Rockefeller tells a small story about his son Michael, who has, he believes, inherited the same quality. As a very young boy Michael fell out of a swing when a rope broke, hit his head on a rock, and was carried into the house seemingly unconscious and very badly hurt. As his mother, his father, and a large and anxious household retinue crowded around him, he opened one eye and remarked, "There seems to be a certain tension in this room."

Rockefeller admires this quality of imperturbability, and although he himself professes to lack it entirely, others, who have watched him assessing a situation with that "sudden narrowing of the eyes," are not so sure. There are some ways, one suspects, in which Rockefeller has deliberately emulated his grandfather (as one also suspects he has deliberately emulated Franklin Roosevelt in others). In Allan Nevins's biography of John D., for example, one comes on such odd characteristics as a "passionate delight . . . in moving and planting trees." Is a passion for moving trees an inheritable characteristic? Or does Nelson Rockefeller have a passion for tree moving because he knows his grandfather did?

There are other, more significant ways in which Nelson Rockefeller is like his grandfather. His grandfather, too, expected the men around him to be "Rockefeller men, first, last, and all the time." But, as Nevins says, he also "wanted everyone in the force to be happy," and he would fuss over his subordinates like a mother hen, meeting the trains of new employees and personally installing them in lodgings of his own choosing. His benevolent paternalism went so far that he required John D. Archbold, his successor as president of Standard Oil, who had a fondness for the hated bottle, to take the pledge—every Sunday thereafter, for some months, a statement signed by Archbold that he had been loyal to his vow was delivered to Rockefeller.

Nelson Rockefeller will go to almost equal lengths in the interests of the "Rockefeller men" around him, doing all sorts of things for them, from prescribing pills for their ailments to quietly subsidizing their children's education. The result is a passionate loyalty among the "happy force" which surrounds Rockefeller. To be sure, there are rare exceptions who are not happy. "I worked for Nelson for two years," one of his former employees recalls, "and then I decided I had to get out or be swallowed up."

But the way in which Rockefeller is most like his grandfather is in their shared faith in what the old man called "method." As Nevins writes, in John D.'s business ventures, "Nothing was guessed at, nothing was left uncounted or unmeasured," and that was perhaps the central secret of his success. To an extent which astonished and mortified his competitors—and destroyed many of them—Rockefeller removed the element of chance from business. When he embarked on an enterprise, it had been studied so carefully and so expertly in advance that there was no reason to guess what would happen. The old man knew what would happen.

No one, as both the ubiquitous Dr. Gallup and a mournful host of political reporters (including this one) discovered in 1948, can safely predict in advance what the unpredictable American voter is really going to do in the voting booth. Even so, so far as it is possible, Nelson Rockefeller, in his new role as a major politician, has from the first applied his grandfather's business methods to the business of politics—and again one suspects that the emulation is quite conscious and deliberate.

Consider the manner of Rockefeller's preparation for the race for the governorship of New York. The preparation began in 1957, well before there was even a whisper of a Rockefeller boom. At that time Rockefeller quietly ordered a series of "studies," as he calls his expert analyses, of his chances of becoming governor. Among those responsible for the studies was one of the most astute of the current crop of pollster-analysts. And Rockefeller had plenty of other expert advisers available—men like Frank Moore, former lieutenant governor of New York under Dewey, who is said to know more about local political situations and personalities than anyone in the state. Before Rockefeller decided to run for governor, Moore had been appointed chairman of the Government Affairs Foundation, a Rockefeller charity.

As a result of his studies, Rockefeller concluded that he had about a two-in-five chance of making it the whole way, and he thereupon decided to make an all-out try for the governorship. Very early, he recruited Judson Morhouse, the supposedly above-the-battle state chairman of the Republican party. Morhouse has recalled how he first became impressed by Rockefeller's political potentialities. The occasion was a 1957 meeting of Republican ladies in Rockefeller's native Westchester County. Rockefeller, who was to address the meeting, had a microphone dangling around his neck. Something went wrong with the apparatus, and Rockefeller's first words came through as a ghastly bellow. Rockefeller dropped the microphone as though it were red hot and asked loudly, in a tone of injured innocence, "Was that me?"

The ladies, joined by Rockefeller, were convulsed by laughter, and although Morhouse says Rockefeller's speech was "terrible," he got a thunderous round of applause when it was over. "That was when I realized this guy had something," Morhouse has said, "and I began to think he might go."

Rockefeller soon found other recruits, notably George Hinman, who had many useful connections, and Malcolm Wilson, now lieutenant governor, a veteran assemblyman and true-blue Republican whose chief role was to reassure the upstate Republican leaders that Rockefeller was a "real Republican." Meanwhile, the making of "studies" never ceased. According to one hardly credible report, there were no less than 134 distinct studies, all connected in one way or another with Rockefeller's gubernatorial prospects and ambitions, made between the time Rockefeller decided to run and his inauguration. Some of these studies were purely political in purpose and effect. For example, Rockefeller-sponsored polls showed Rockefeller running behind Governor Averell Harriman by a seemingly disastrous 60–40 ratio. But they also showed Rockefeller running well ahead of Leonard Hall and the other Republican candidates for the nomination. These polls were used by Morhouse to persuade the upstate leaders not to commit themselves prematurely.

Other Rockefeller studies were designed to prepare Rockefeller for his job as governor (and some of these were undertaken, mind you, when his own polls gave Harriman a three-to-two lead over him). The result was that as soon as he was inaugurated Rockefeller was ready with an ambitious legislative program, including new and bold formulas for dealing with New York's horrendous housing and commuting problems. Another result, of course, was to give him a solid basis for judging the issues to hit hardest in his campaign against Harriman.

It was a smooth-as-silk operation from start to finish, and what Rockefeller's grandfather called "method" was employed with triumphant success throughout. From heaven— if that is where he is—old John D. must have beamed down on his grandson, in his first try as a serious politician, leaving "nothing guessed at, nothing uncounted or unmeasured." And yet the old man, for all his genius, could not possibly have done what his grandson did. For if there are ways in which grandfather and grandson are startlingly alike, there is at least one way in which they are absolutely different. And the difference explains why one of the most hated men of one generation produced, at one remove, one of the most popular politicians of another generation.

That "untouched quality," the curious imperturbability which Nelson Rockefeller admired in his grandfather, was one reason why the old man was so hated. With his skull-like face, wholly without hair (all the hair fell out of his body in his forties), it was easy to picture the old man as an inhuman monster, a "behemoth," an "anaconda," crushing the life out of his innocent victims without a flicker of human emotion. As Nevins wrote, "His want of warmth and likability cost Rockefeller dear."

"Warmth and likability" are Nelson Rockefeller's most striking superficial characteristics. Without those characteristics, however brilliant his "method," however carefully he had measured and counted and studied and analyzed the political situation, Nelson Rockefeller could not possibly have been nominated, much less elected, to the governorship of New York. In the contest for the nomination, the Rockefeller charm was a key factor. According to Morhouse, it was so overpowering that when Rockefeller went upstate to visit the Republican leaders, "the guys would swoon—we had ecstatic reports coming in from all over." And there is no question that the Rockefeller warmth and likability, which contrasted with the faintly ducal manner of his opponent, Averell Harriman, were the qualities that elected him. They are also the qualities which could make him a serious rival to Richard Nixon, and even the next occupant of the White House.

Where, then, did Nelson Rockefeller acquire these qualities which his paternal grandfather so notably lacked? Part of the answer is that he was trained to have them, as a race horse is trained to speed and endurance. Another part of the answer is that he inherited them. For Nelson Rockefeller, like most human beings, had two grandfathers.

The other one, Senator Nelson Aldrich of Rhode Island, is almost forgotten now. But he was a very big mover and shaker in his own day. In the last ten years of his thirty years in the Senate, Aldrich was the dominant figure in that august body. He was, in some ways, the Robert A. Taft of his generation—the recognized spokesman of the conservative interest and, rather briefly, the leader of the conservative Republican opposition to Theodore Roosevelt. But unlike Taft, and very much unlike John D. Rockefeller, he was also a gay old dog. Through the mists of time, a dim but congenial picture of the old senator emerges—a witty and exuberant fellow with a taste for good wine, pretty women, fine horses, and good pictures. He was a natural-born politician and, like most natural-born politicians, an immensely likable man.

There is certainly a lot of the old senator in that other natural-born politician, his grandson. There is certainly also a lot of his daughter and Nelson's mother, Abby Aldrich Rockefeller, whom Mr. Junior married after a long and singularly unimpulsive courtship. Abby Rockefeller, who died in 1948, was a charming woman, by all accounts, whom Nelson adored and in many ways resembles. She was also his principal mentor in achieving those characteristics of "warmth and likability."

In Mary Ellen Chase's engaging biography of Abby Rockefeller, a rather fascinating correspondence appears. The letters were first published in the *Atlantic Monthly* in 1919 and 1929, the first written by an irritated neighbor of the Rockefellers, the reply (which was no doubt received with amazement by the *Atlantic* editors) by Abby Rockefeller. The letters are worth reproducing in full, for they tell a great deal about the unique circumstances of Nelson Rockefeller's upbringing.

My dear Mr. Aristos,—

Since you moved into this neighborhood and bought a thousand acres of land, we have lived within five hundred feet of one another for seven years. Your lady and I exchange calls and have long pleasant chats. Our children lunch together at each other's houses; we accept each other's invitations to dinner, and I think we all four enjoy these occasions. The boys and girls exchange proffers of outdoor sports to be enjoyed together; though yours seldom accept because they are too busy with lessons, and so ours are sparing of their own acceptances.

Certain privileges of wood and water which we enjoyed before you created your estate, we continue to enjoy with your courteous encouragement and apparently to your entire satisfaction. You also offer to sell us vegetables at low rates, or to give us kindling from the enormous piles of packing-boxes which accumulate in your back premises from time to time; and you do various other little acts, trying to help make life agreeable for us.

When we asked you to sell us a parcel of land—sixty by seventy feet—which we had not been able to secure from the former owner, in order to complete our precious three acres, you offered us the free use of that bit "just as if it were ours, without payment" saying that you disliked ever to part with any land.

When we heard you were coming near us, we were troubled, for we feared the close neighborhood of elaborateness and formality and pride. We were afraid our children might have to learn that there is arrogance even in America. But not so. You are simple. You are kind. You have been in every way a good neighbor, a remarkably good neighbor.

It is curious that, after seven years of such perfectly friendly intercourse, we are not friends. We know a great deal more about each other than we did in the beginning; but we do not really know each other any better at all. This is the more odd, because we have so many points of agreement in matters which make the most difference between folks. A sense of duty is the leading emotion in your lives as well as in ours. You are sincere; you, too, are interested in social betterment, and in educational improvement; you like the same sports. We all four enjoy the same magazines (the *Atlantic* being the sole reading of any one of us sometimes for weeks), and we admire the same public men. Your land is just like ours, only there is more of it. Your house has the same appointments as ours, only there are more of them and they are finer. We all wear the same kind of clothes, only you have more of them. Each couple loves its own children more than anything else except, of course, each other. We all admire and cultivate the same kind of manners; we even enjoy the same kind of jokes. What more is necessary to make people friends?

And yet, we are not friends. As I see it, the explanation is *your money*,—your extra money,—not the money you spend, but the money you have not spent.

We are so afraid that you will think we are after it, that we dare not talk freely on any of the subjects which interest us most deeply—because those subjects are all *objects;* and *objects* always need money. You are so redundantly rich! Whatever one of our dreams we might begin to be eloquent about, we could not long conceal the fact that it was still but a little way toward fulfillment—for lack of money. In short, whatever we said, we should consciously fear that we sounded like beggars. And beggars, satellites, or dependents, we will not be. We have a fixed determination not to ask money for any of our projects from people who are not already eager to give.

And on your side, we are utterly at a loss to know how you feel. We have an impression that we do not seem to you of the slightest importance. Your refusing to sell the strip of land to us seemed to us equivalent to saying, "We do not care to make you at home near us. We think of you as of birds who have nested close by. We treat you with consideration, and we watch you with interest, but we shall not care when you flit, leaving the nest empty and ourselves more free to range at pleasure beneath your trees."

Nothing you ever say or do seems to prove anything different. There is, indeed, a possibility that you are as diffident as we. Perhaps you like us as fully as we like you, but are afraid that we do not find you interesting. But no! A rich man practically always looks upon a man who has not made money as a failure, unless he has gained fame. Even then, he inclines to doubt the value of a fame which cannot gain financial recognition. As a matter of fact, are you not all the while silently on the watch to avoid encroachments from us, and to elude possible openings for favors to be asked? Are you not all the time on guard against our becoming beggars, satellites, or dependents?

And so it goes; we take the privileges of wood and water, because we believe that in a properly conducted state these opportunities would be ours of public right. We do not take other favors which you offer, because we believe that in a properly conducted state those things would still be matters of private right, and we have no special claim upon you. We have not the claim of friendship, which is the only basis upon which one can accept private favors. In a friendship, the exchange of invisible benefits is so great, so constant, and so valuable, that tangible benefits are given and received without consideration of money value, simply as outward expressions of that inner interchange.

Do you remember that, several years ago, after we had once or twice invited your boys to go sailing or snowshoeing with us, you offered to employ my husband to take charge of their sports all the time? So it goes. You look upon us as a duty, and as a possible convenience, but never, it seems to us, as possible friends. We are sorry, for we like you candidly, and you are our nearest neighbors.

Yours cordially,
Your Friend and Neighbor

P.S. I cannot send you this letter, because you might think it sheer impudence; or, if you did not, any efforts which you made thereafter to become friends would seem to us to spring from your all-pervasive sense of duty, and we should give them a cold reception as being favors which we had asked for. We will not be beggars.

To the Editor of the *Atlantic Monthly*.

It is seldom that an unsent letter reaches its destination. As this one was received through your columns, may it not be answered in the same way? For your information, may I say that I am the wife of the "Very Rich Neighbor."

My dear Neighbor:

I agree with you that we are not intimate friends, though friends I had felt we were. I do not agree with you, however, as to the cause.

Your "Rich Neighbor" gives ten months of the year unreservedly to the task of administering his stewardship to the end that the wealth entrusted to his care may bring enlarged opportunity, health, happiness and comfort to his fellow men. His wife is his ardent supporter and feeble imitator.

The two months which he spends as your neighbor give him his only opportunity to play. During this time his aim is to become intimate with his children, to read the books he longs to read, to exercise out of doors, to get near to Nature, to have time to think, to meditate, to plan; in other words, to refresh his spirit. At such a time it is not that one does not want to see one's friends;

it is simply that to be worth while to one's friends and the cause of righteousness, one must—so to speak—retire into the wilderness. Moreover, during this vacation there are duties which interfere with a greater interchange of social visits, such as an enormous mail which persists in coming and must be answered. Under the circumstances, the mere fact that your "Rich Neighbor" prefers to spend his mornings chopping wood or riding and playing tennis with his boys, his afternoons driving or walking—he and I together—his evenings with the children, inevitably results in but little time remaining. It may seem selfish, but it has nothing to do with money.

Admiring your husband immensely, we sought for our boys his companionship. To offer compensation for his added responsibility seemed only fair.

Why my husband did not sell you the strip of land, I do not remember. I suspect, being mere man, he simply didn't want to. It was entirely impersonal.

Most rich people seem unresponsive, but it is not entirely their fault; they are not treated naturally. My husband and I were once asked to a simple home where I know they had delicious baked beans; we were treated to poor roast chicken. The rich are given what they are expected to want, both intellectually and gastronomically. It may be flattering but it is not stimulating or wholesome. A sense of humor and a good mind may be hidden beneath a tiara.

To their faces the rich are often accorded a respect that is not felt, and behind their backs a contempt that is not deserved.

Please, dear neighbor and dear reader, too, help the deserving rich by not taking us too seriously and by forgetting that surplus money.

Sincerely,
"Mrs. Aristos"

As the letter from "Mrs. Aristos" suggests, Abby Rockefeller was a thoroughly literate and even witty woman. She was what the Rockefellers so markedly were not, exuberant and gay. "I confess," she wrote one of her sons, "if I had my way, I really think I should like to give a party every day." She was also, according to contemporaries, a woman with a whim of iron, and she was determined to bring up her six children in such a way that they would be "treated naturally," and so that people really would "forget all that surplus money." To that end, she trained her daughter and her five sons to be, quite simply, nice to other people.

Her letters to them are full of such admonitions as: "Old people like to be made a part of things. Don't forget to go out of your way to make them feel wanted and at home." Or, of a homesick schoolmate: "I hope you will take pains to get acquainted right away. I hate to think of him homesick and sad." Or: "What I would like you always to do is what I try humbly to do myself; that is, never say or do anything which would wound the feelings or the self-respect of any human being, and to give special consideration to all who are in any way repressed."

All the third-generation Rockefellers show the effects of this early training in the art of being nice. But the training took best with Nelson, the most naturally gregarious and likable of the lot in any case. Just how well the training took is suggested by the picture of Nelson in college which emerges from the recollections of his classmates and instructors. Here, for example, is a Dartmouth professor who knew him well:

"When he came to my house, he behaved exactly as though he came from a well-organized, relaxed, middle-class family. He'd go into the kitchen after supper and help with the dishes without a trace of self-consciousness, as though he always did the same things in his own house—maybe he did, for all I know. I remember his telling my wife the best silver polish was something called Oakite—saved a lot of work, he said."

Excerpts from some of the more interesting letters from Rockefeller's classmates to the author are to be found in the appendix, and those who want to judge for themselves the impression he made on his classmates should examine them. But there is no doubt at all of the basic impression he made —he was universally considered "a wonderful guy" and a "regular fellow." Here are a few sentences which convey this impression:

"He is the same wonderful fellow he has always been, and we all love him." "In his whole college career, Nelson was 'one of the boys.'" "His normal appearance—crew cut, dirty corduroy pants and a green sweater—was as sloppy, if not more so, than the college average." "He was always so outgoing and cheerful it was impossible not to like him." "Nelson won many honors, scholastically and socially, but he won them on merit." "He had and apparently still has the personality of a natural politician." "He wanted to be accepted as a 'regular guy.'" "He was just thoroughly wholesome in a very masculine way."

He was intelligent, but not immoderately so—— "In his studies," writes his former roommate, John French, "he was a hard, conscientious (though not brilliant) worker, with an inquiring mind." He was a good soccer player, but no standout as an athlete. He was earnest and highly moral—he taught Sunday school and "did not swear, smoke, or drink," as became a Rockefeller. On the other hand, as became an Aldrich, he enjoyed practical jokes and "loved a good rough-house." He was on a modest allowance, and he was rather pinchpenny. "The price of our fraternity picture was fifty cents unframed and a dollar framed. . . . Nelson said he would take it unframed for he could frame it himself for less than fifty cents."

It was toward the end of his college career that Rockefeller began to be interested in art. That was a downright eccentric interest in the Dartmouth of those days, for Dartmouth was very much of a he-man college, known at the time as having "the biggest gymnasium and the smallest library in the East." And yet the one really noteworthy and original thing that Rockefeller did in college was to revive a moldering organization called The Arts, which, as he wrote at the time, "had dropped into disrepute several years ago as it had come into the hands of a group of light-footed tea drinkers, at least so rumor has it."

If Rockefeller had not been so obvious a he-man and a regular fellow, he might have been suspected of being a light-footed tea drinker himself. Instead, as Churchill Lathrop, a Dartmouth professor, has testified, art became "socially accepted" at Dartmouth because of Rockefeller. And as Rockefeller himself wrote, "The Arts came back into its own on campus stronger than ever."

Rockefeller arranged for visits to the campus of various intellectuals—Thornton Wilder, Bertrand Russell, Edna St. Vincent Millay—and he sponsored a poetry contest and music recitals. But his real interest was in painting. He dabbled a bit in painting himself, and he imported "excellent reproductions made by a new German process" to the campus. He hoped, as he wrote at the time, "to encourage fellows to buy worthwhile pictures for their rooms, rather than spend the same amount of money for poor stuff as many of them do." Despite the crass commercial note in this remark, Rockefeller's interest in art was perfectly real, and it has lasted all his life, as we have seen.

The story of Rockefeller and The Arts suggests a question: Was there an intellectual lurking well concealed behind that old green sweater? The answer appears to be that there was not. Rockefeller was, and is, intelligent, and his aestheticism was, and is, real. But like most natural-born politicians, he is a pragmatist, with a certain contempt for those involved in ideas rather than action. He very rarely reads a book, although he is often "briefed" on a book which his staff considers important. On the other hand, he does not have the contempt for and suspicion of intellectuals that Harry Truman and Dwight Eisenhower shared. Again, in this respect, he is like Franklin Roosevelt who, though no intellectual himself, enjoyed the company of intellectuals and liked to pick their brains.

Aside from his eccentric interest in The Arts, the picture that emerges of Nelson Rockefeller in his college days is of a boy unremarkable in every way except one—he was remarkably likable. There is no doubt at all that he was one of the two or three best-liked boys in his class, and that his popularity had nothing to do with his money. In every other way, he was almost ostentatiously ordinary. And surely this is rather mysterious, that the unique circumstances of his upbringing, the vast wealth, the enormous estates, the hated name, and all the rest of it should produce a likable, seemingly ordinary young man, a regular guy in an old green sweater.

It happened that way because it was planned that way. Nelson Rockefeller represents the extraordinary trained to appear ordinary. His classmates recall a story about the battered old wreck of a car Rockefeller owned in his senior year. A friend asked him why he didn't sell it and get something more respectable. "What do you think I am," Rockefeller is supposed to have replied, "a Vanderbilt?"

The story is probably apocryphal—the same story, more or less, was told about his father when he was young. But like many apocryphal stories it has a valid point. By Abby Rockefeller and by their father, too, the third-generation Rockefellers were trained rigorously to avoid Vanderbiltian airs.[1] A Rockefeller was trained to be a "regular guy" or "one of

---

[1] *The Vanderbilts, in the early days, looked down on the Rockefellers as new rich, just as the Astors had looked down on the Vanderbilts and the Stuyvesants and Van Rensselaers on the Astors, and so on throughout the silly story of America's fake aristocracy.*

the boys" as carefully as the scions of other rich American families were trained to adopt a ducal air. The training took well with all six children. But Nelson Rockefeller is certainly the most triumphant end product of Abby Rockefeller's determination that her children would be so natural that they would be "treated naturally" and "all that surplus money" would be forgotten.

The surplus money cannot ever really be forgotten, of course. When Abby Rockefeller and Mr. Junior went to Dartmouth to see Nelson, they always visited all his instructors. "They were as nice and easy as they could be," one Dartmouth professor recalls. "But they published big incomes in those days, and I figured out that in the time it took Mrs. Rockefeller to drink a cup of my wife's tea, Mr. Rockefeller was richer by a sum bigger than my whole year's salary."

The surplus money is not forgotten today, any more than it was then. Everyone who meets him is always, inevitably, aware of that invisible dollar sign dangling over Nelson Rockefeller's head. And yet Abby Rockefeller's training in the art of being nice—plus, of course, those genes she passed on to him from her genial politician father—have transformed the dollar sign from the total political liability it would have been not long ago into at least a dubious political asset. Because most people do not expect a very rich man to be likable, Nelson Rockefeller's likability is multiplied by his money.

Both Nelson Rockefeller's grandfathers, the great capitalist and the Senate leader, were remarkable men, and the circumstances of his upbringing were even more remarkable. Any amateur student of the combined effects of heredity and environment would confidently predict that such a combination should produce something rather extraordinary.

The five Rockefeller brothers are all able men in their own ways, but judging from the record, Nelson is the only one who deserves the label extraordinary. And perhaps the most extraordinary thing about him is that to most people he does not seem extraordinary at all. He seems "a wonderful guy" or "a regular fellow" or "as comfortable as an old shoe" or—to revert to Nixon's unpleasant phrase—"a buddy-buddy boy." Nixon himself, for all his ability and intelligence, is almost as incapable as was Nelson Rockefeller's paternal grandfather of appearing to be a "buddy-buddy boy" or "as comfortable as an old shoe." And that is why it still seems possible, as this is written, that Nixon will at last feel the great prize for which he has worked so hard and long slipping from his grasp.

If the climax of the Rockefeller drama should ever be the election of Nelson Rockefeller to the presidency of the United States, a lot of people could take a bow after the curtain had rung down. But when the subsidiary players in the drama, people like Morhouse and Hinman and Harrison, had gracefully retired, Rockefeller would be left alone on the stage with four oddly assorted ghosts—his mother, his two grandfathers, and Franklin D. Roosevelt.

7

How They Got That Way: Nixon

An attempt to put into a single sentence the most important facts about Nixon's background might read as follows: "Richard Milhous Nixon, a Black Irishman from a poor but pious Quaker family, was brought up in a small town near Hollywood, California."

As previously noted, Nixon and Rockefeller both had an exceedingly pious upbringing, and they share, as a result, a certain moral fervor which makes those who dislike them, dislike them the more. But in many other ways the circumstances to which they were born were, of course, totally dissimilar.

Rockefeller is mostly English and Dutch. Nixon is mostly Irish, on both sides. He is no ordinary Irish American, to be sure. For one thing, he is not a Catholic. For another, instead of arriving at the time of the potato famine in the nineteenth century, his Irish ancestors arrived in the eighteenth century, when there was hardly any Irish immigration at all. The first Nixon landed in Delaware from Ireland before 1750, and the first Milhous came over from County Kildare even earlier.

Nixon's Irish blood is not undiluted by this time. But the Irish tend to marry the Irish—Nixon boasted of the Irish blood of his wife, born Thelma Ryan, in the fund speech—and Nixon's essential Irishness is indisputable.

You only have to look at the man, moreover, to see that he falls into the special category of the "Black Irish"—the Irish whose Iberian bloodlines show through in black hair and dark coloring. The fact that he is Irish—and Black Irish to boot—tells a lot about Nixon. The Black Irish have the reputation of being even more ready to fight at the drop of a hat than most Irish, and anyone who has ever done any experimental pub crawling in New York's Irish bars will testify that the reputation is justified.[1]

Put a clay pipe in Nixon's mouth and a hod on his shoulder or a shillelagh in his hand, and there, complete with beetling brows and uptilted nose, is the original of the old cartoon stereotype of the fighting Irishman—the Irishman of the draft riots or of *Punch's* version of the Sinn Feiner. "I believe in hitting back," Nixon says, in defense of some of his past excesses. "When someone attacks, my instinct is to strike back." That is a thoroughly Irish instinct.

But Nixon is a Quaker as well as a Black Irishman. That must be, surely, an uncomfortable combination to live with.

---

[1] *No doubt it is most unscientific to suppose that those of Irish ancestry have any special characteristics, but, to paraphrase Mr. Bumble on the law, if science believes that, science is an ass.*

On the one hand, the hot Irish "instinct to strike back." On the other, the teaching of the Society of Friends that violence is abhorrent, that the other cheek must always be turned. The Quakerism of Nixon's youth was no casual matter, moreover. Both his great-grandmother and his great-great-grandmother on his mother's side were well-known itinerant lady preachers. Nixon's maternal grandmother, a determined old lady who wrote inspirational verse and dominated the family in Nixon's boyhood, was very religious. So was his mother, a charming elderly lady who looks like Whistler's mother with a ski-jump nose. Both his mother and his grandmother hoped that Richard (they never called him "Dick") would be a famous preacher like his forebears. The Nixon family, in short, took their religion at least as seriously as the Rockefellers took theirs.

The strange combination—the prim Quaker upbringing and the hot Irish instinct to hit back—is important to an understanding of Nixon. So is the fact that the Nixon family was of the respectable poor.

How poor were the Nixons? The answer seems to be that they were the kind of family who were poor by most standards, but who never thought of themselves as poor. There was serious illness in the family—two Nixon brothers died young —and meeting doctors' bills was a major problem. Hand-me-downs, hard work, and not much fun—that was the pattern of Nixon's boyhood. It seems likely that a strong urge to escape from that pattern had something to do with Nixon's tremendous ambition. "There was a drive to succeed; to survive, almost," Nixon says, as though survival and success were almost equivalents.

His mother and father, as he also says, certainly had something to do with that drive. His mother is a woman of genuine charm—"Everybody always loved Hannah Nixon" is a phrase you are likely to hear in Whittier, the Nixon home town. Not everybody loved the late Frank Nixon, Nixon's father. Frank

Nixon, who died in 1956, was a cantankerous fellow who suf-
fered from bleeding ulcers most of his life, and who liked
nothing better than an argument. He must have been a remarkable fellow in his way. Jessamyn West, author of *The
Friendly Persuasion* and a cousin of Nixon's, recalls Frank
Nixon, who taught Sunday school, as follows:

"Frank was not only the best Sunday school teacher I ever
had, he was just about the best teacher. Frank had the prime
requisite for teaching: great enthusiasm for his subject; and
he always aroused in his pupils a like enthusiasm. . . . He
related his Sunday school lessons to life about us, to politics,
local and national. His class was so popular it overflowed the
space allotted to it and if I could have attended it a few more
years I think I might have become a fair stateswoman myself."

Despite his brilliance as a teacher, Frank Nixon, to borrow
the current cant of sociologists, achieved only "limited success status"—his various attempts to earn a living, as a motor-
man, lemon grower, and storekeeper, were never really
successful. To keep it a going concern, the whole family had
to work in the store, which was the family's main source of
income when Nixon was a boy. Hannah was a Milhous, and
the Milhouses were among the early arrivals when Whittier
was founded in the late nineteenth century. As a member of
one of the founding families, Hannah was rather widely regarded in Whittier as having made an unfortunate marriage
—which is no doubt one reason why Frank Nixon was so
combative. His own "competitive characteristic," Nixon says,
"goes back to my dad."

The fact that Whittier is not much more than a stone's
throw from Hollywood is also worth noting. Southern California (like Texas or New England or the Deep South, or for
that matter any part of the United States you care to name)
bequeaths to its native sons certain special attitudes and
standards of value, and in southern California Hollywood
has a good deal to do with those attitudes and standards. If

Nixon had been a native of New Hampshire, say, or Iowa, he might have said essentially what he did say in the famous fund speech, but it seems safe to suppose that he would have said it in a different way.

Nixon's Irishness, his Quaker upbringing, his family circumstances, and his southern California background are the essential reference points in an attempt to understand the man. To see a little deeper, to get a surer glimpse of what lies beneath the Nixon carapace, it is necessary to go to Whittier, to sense the atmosphere of the place, and to talk to the people who knew the boy who was the father of the man. It is a fascinating experience.

Whittier is a most agreeable place, basking in almost permanent sunshine, marred only occasionally by smog. Founded by Quakers like the Milhous family, it was named after the "good gray poet," John Greenleaf Whittier. The Quakers are now heavily outnumbered, but there is still a Quakerish smell to the place—it is neat but not gaudy, without slums, without external evidence of great wealth. The architecture is pleasantly typical of what an English lady has called "America's Lily Cup architecture—use once and throw away." Everything in the town seems to have been built yesterday, or at most the day before. As throughout southern California, one has the feeling that the past influences the present less than anywhere in the world. The slate has been wiped clean, and what matters is not yesterday, but prosperous today, and even more prosperous tomorrow.

Whittier is small enough so that you can see most of the people who knew Nixon well in a few days. The best friend of his boyhood is a successful automobile dealer who probably makes about twice as much money as the Vice-President, and whose admiration for Nixon is so fervent that his eyes fill with tears when he is talking about him. You can find the boy whom Nixon defeated, in an election for the presidency of the student body of Whittier College, behind the counter of a local clothing shop—a pleasant fellow, who looks a good deal younger than Nixon (and who may well be a good deal happier). Nixon's mother lives close by, and so do most of the people who taught him at school and college. Talking to such people, that ghost from the past, Nixon the boy, begins to take on flesh and blood, and an oddly interesting boy he turns out to be.

Even the simple, recorded facts of Nixon's early life tell something about him, of course. His school and college records have a Horatio Alger consistency. In Whittier High School he was first in his class scholastically, a champion debater, and the loser by a hair in a contest for the class presidency (it was the only time in his life Nixon ever lost an election). In Whittier College he was second in his class, president of the student body, a champion debater, and a very bad football player. At Duke University Law School in North Carolina—he went there on a scholarship and was graduated in 1937—he was third in his class, the equivalent of president of the student body, and on the law review.

Obviously the boy Nixon was intelligent—his scholastic record proves it. Obviously he was popular—an unpopular boy is not regularly elected to office by his fellow students. Obviously he had a strong political instinct even then—a boy who is not politically minded does not run for office every chance he gets. But what kind of boy was Richard Nixon really?

Trying to answer that question is a fascinating pastime, rather like that old favorite of children's birthday parties in which the eager player follows a string around and about and over and under until he comes at last on the hidden prize. For again and again the digger into Nixon's past comes upon something in the nature of the boy which leads directly, in a flash of recognition, to something in the nature of the man.

Recall, for example, the passage which, aside from the immortal Checkers, most people remember best from the fund speech: "I should say this, that Pat doesn't have a mink coat, but she does have a respectable Republican cloth coat, and I always tell her she'd look good in anything."

Now open the 1934 edition of the annual yearbook of Whittier College to page 88, and from it you will see, peering out self-consciously, the faces of the twenty-eight members of the Franklin Society. Every Franklin is clad in the unaccustomed splendor of a tuxedo. Turn the page, and you find the twenty-seven members of the Orthogonian Society, the rivals of the Franklins. Every Orthogonian is dressed in a simple white shirt, sleeves rolled up, collars open over boyish throats. Comparing the two, one cannot help feeling that the Orthogonians are somehow more natural, more likable—if you will, more American—than the aristocratically garbed Franklins.

Among the Orthogonians you recognize the familiar face —the ski-jump nose is there already and the jowls are beginning faintly to appear—of Richard Milhous Nixon, founder and first president of the Orthogonian Society. Most of the Orthogonians, who were on the average poorer than the long-established Franklins, could not afford in those depression years to rent, much less to own, tuxedos. So founder-president Nixon made a virtue of necessity, as he was so often to do as politician Nixon. It was his idea to have the Orthogonians photographed in simple, democratic, open shirts, thus dramatizing the contrast with the hifalutin Franklins.

The parallel between those open shirts and the "respectable Republican cloth coat" is quite obvious, and Nixon himself is well aware of it. When, in the talk reproduced in the appendix, this reporter remarked that he thought he had found the origins of the Republican cloth coat in a Whittier yearbook, Nixon chuckled, with instant recognition: "Sure, sure, the open collars. They were the haves and we were the have nots, see. I was just a freshman then."

Obviously freshman Nixon shared with politician Nixon

an unerring instinct for political symbolism, and an instinct also for turning seeming misfortune to advantage. Or take another example of the sudden sense of recognition which rewards the digger into Nixon's past. Nixon tried out for football every year at Whittier. He was slight and ill-coordinated, and although in four years he was never late for practice, he never made the team. He was useful chiefly as a kind of tireless, indestructible, animated ninepin for the better players to knock down. "He was a lousy player but he sure had guts," recalls the automobile salesman, a Whittier College football star in his day. Once in a long while Nixon would be permitted to play in the last few minutes of a game. When that happened, recalls a classmate who was football linesman at the time, "I always got out the five-yard penalty marker. Dick was so eager that I knew he'd be offside just about every play."

Nixon has unquestionably been "offside" more than once in his subsequent career. This is not the place to recite the case against Nixon—that will come in the next chapter. The purpose here is to try to understand the kind of man Nixon is by trying to understand the kind of boy he was. One thing that was true of Nixon the boy, as it is of Nixon the man, is a curious ambivalence, a sort of inner contradiction, between that drive and overeagerness which took him "offside just about every play" and a highly moral, even a moralistic, attitude. Is it the Black Irishman and the Quaker in him? Or is it his cantankerous father and his gently pious mother, alternately triumphing?

The interested reader can find echoes of this internal contradiction in some of the letters from his classmates printed in the appendix. Here, for example, is a classmate who recalled charges that Nixon as a politician had used "questionable tactics": "He was a man of such high ambition, and a man capable of pursuing his ambition with such intensity, that I could the more easily believe that he would and could do whatever was necessary to attain the goal he had set for himself. However, I have serious doubts whether he himself did those things, because I got the impression of Richard, in college, that he had very high morals and was motivated largely by a very high sense of duty."

Nothing more irritates Nixon's enemies, especially the more cynical and sophisticated, than the "very high morals" and the "very high sense of duty." It was the "holier-than-thou" note in the famous fund speech which infuriated such people more than anything else in the speech. The first sentence, with its overtones of injured righteousness, set the tone: "My fellow Americans, I come before you tonight as a candidate for the vice-presidency and as a man whose honesty and integrity have been questioned."

His enemies are convinced—just as the first John D. Rockefeller's enemies were convinced—that Nixon's high moral outlook is sheer hypocrisy. But remember those lady preachers who were Nixon's forebears, and remember his mother, who hoped that little Richard would be a preacher, too. Remember the moralistic atmosphere of the Nixon household, which is suggested by a story of Nixon as a little boy which his mother tells with pride. It was at the time of the Teapot Dome scandals, and little Richard, a great newspaper reader even then, was sprawled in front of the fire reading about the awful goings on in Washington. He turned to her and announced: "I know what I want to be when I grow up—an honest lawyer who doesn't cheat people but helps them."

Again and again one catches echoes of that early announcement, with its faintly priggish note of high moral principle. When Nixon was "just a freshman" at Whittier College, the Franklin Society was the only men's club on the campus, and its comparative handful of members enjoyed all the special delights which such a social monopoly entails. Nixon, whose reputation as a coming man had preceded him from high school, was almost immediately asked to join. He refused—

on principle. The Franklins' social monopoly was, he held, unfair and contrary to the democratic spirit. But having thus acted on principle, he at once became highly practical and competitive and organized, in the Orthogonians, a successful rival club, which must have been quite a trick for a mere freshman.

This succession—a gesture on principle immediately followed by a highly practical and successful subsequent course —is repeated rather often. When Nixon was a young lawyer with OPA at the beginning of the war, he insisted on taking the lowest possible salary. "He reasoned," writes his chief of the OPA days, Professor Jacob Buescher, "that the boys who were being trained to hit the beaches were paid a lot less." But having made this noble gesture, it was typical of Nixon that he rapidly ascended from his self-imposed low rung on the bureaucratic ladder.

In college Nixon was a very model boy. He neither smoked nor drank—although by the time he went to law school he had relaxed sufficiently to sip an occasional beer. Aside from the usual nonsense of painting outhouses on rival campuses, and the like, the only youthful escapade his contemporaries recall involved his crawling over the transom to get into the dean's office in law school. But his purpose was not to boobytrap the dean's desk, or some such shenanigans. It was to discover, from the dean's records, where he stood scholastically.

As this episode suggests, those other qualities in Nixon, his "ambition and intensity," were very much a part of the boy, as they are of the man. As Nixon says, both his parents taught him to try to be "good, not just at one thing, but at everything," and he certainly tried hard, as he has been trying ever since. And although he was a very bad football player, he was good at almost everything else.

He was a good actor, for example. Dr. Albert Upton, his drama coach, has recalled a play in which Nixon, as a sadly bereft old innkeeper, was to appear alone on the stage, weeping. "I told him, 'Dick, if you just concentrate real hard on getting a big lump in your throat, I think you can cry real tears.' He did, too—buckets of tears. I couldn't help remembering the play when I saw that picture of Dick crying on Senator Knowland's shoulder. But mind you, Dick is never spurious, he really felt it."

Again, consider the fund speech. Nixon's enemies are convinced—and again nothing on earth will dissuade them—that the highly emotional tone of the speech was as spurious as the note of moral virtue. But consider Nixon's circumstances. Here was an enormously ambitious young man who saw his whole career threatened with total and irrecoverable ruin. Here, too, was the young man with the Quaker upbringing who had told his mother that he wanted to be a "good lawyer who doesn't cheat," the young man who had always been regarded in school and college as a paragon of virtue and honor, and had so regarded himself. And here he was, held up before the nation as a scoundrel ready to sell out to a group of wealthy men for a few thousand dollars.

Of course Nixon's emotion was real—if it had been wholly spurious, Nixon would not have been human. It was the way in which the emotion was conveyed that was spurious—above all, the immortal hamminess of the "little cocker spaniel dog" which "Tricia, the six-year-old, named Checkers." But Nixon, remember, was brought up almost within shouting distance of Hollywood, and in his part of California hamminess was, and is, a way of life, and a highly respected one.

It is interesting also to re-read the fund speech, as well as other Nixon pronouncements, in light of the fact that Nixon was a college debater. He was more than good at debating he was brilliant, the champion debater of southern California. Debating was taken seriously at Whittier, as in many western colleges, and being president of the debate team automatically made Nixon a very big man on the campus. The Reverend William Hornaday, now a well-known preacher in Los

Angeles, and in those days Nixon's debating teammate, recalls the advice of Professor Eugene Knox, their debating coach—"Never throw your arms about, keep your elbows close in to your stomach." When Nixon makes a speech today, it is easy to see him still following that advice.

There are other very evident carry-overs from Nixon the college debater to Nixon the major politician. Hornaday recalls how shrewd and longheaded Nixon was in debate. "He used to pass me little notes, 'Pour it on at this point,' or 'Save your ammunition,' or 'Play to the judges, they're the ones who decide.'" His high-school debating coach, a lady and a Democrat, remembers, "He was so good it kind of disturbed me. He had this ability to kind of slide round an argument, instead of meeting it head on, and he could take any side of a debate." Those qualities of Nixon, as a youthful debater, are also worth bearing in mind.

Hornaday, a well-regarded marimba player in his college days, still has a note from Nixon, scrawled in his classbook in a rather childish hand: "You are a great musician, Delyn. But I will remember you as a friend, a brother, and a splendid politician. Yours, Dick Nixon." Even more than as a debater, it was as a "splendid politician"—perhaps the most successful politician ever to appear on the campus—that Nixon scored most heavily at Whittier. The Whittier yearbook has a full-page picture of Nixon, looking very young and very purposeful, as president of the student body, and below is the paragraph:

"After one of the most successful years the college has ever witnessed, we stop to reminisce, and come to the realization that much of the success was due to the efforts of this very gentleman. Always progressive, and with a liberal attitude, he has led us through the year with flying colors."

On the opposite page is an account of Nixon's political triumph: "After a fairly quiet political season, and a campaign in which mudslinging was notably absent, the student body chose its officers for the year. Although political dictators managed to cause as much trouble as possible, Dick Nixon came through the melee unscathed with the title of student-body president. On a platform advocating a new deal for those who enjoy the social niceties, he stormed to his position."

The "social niceties" were on-campus dances, previously outlawed on that Quaker campus. Nixon disliked dancing then, and dislikes it to this day, but he clearly had a well-developed instinct for the winning issue, even then.

The odd fact is that, although they kept electing him to office, most of his classmates did not think of Nixon as a natural politician at all. "He was the last person in the class I would have picked for a political headline," one law-school classmate wrote; and another: "I would put him down as the man least likely to succeed in politics."

Most Americans think of a politician as a "buddy-buddy boy," to revert to Nixon's horrible phrase, and Nixon was not then, any more than he is now, a "buddy-buddy boy." That is another note his contemporaries repeatedly strike in their letters about Nixon. "He was personally somewhat shy." . . . "Definitely not an extrovert." . . . "Basically aloof, very sure of himself, and very careful to keep people from getting too close to him." . . . "He was not what you would call a real friendly guy." . . . "He tended somewhat to shyness."

Yet his classmates liked him. One lady recalls that she "thought Dick Nixon was too stuck-up." She was an exception; Nixon did not then have the genius he has since displayed for making enemies. But very few of his classmates felt really close to him. In the Whittier yearbook a most revealing cartoon appears. The members of the class are portrayed, in various informal attitudes, chatting and laughing with each other. In the center of the picture, and dominating the composition, is Richard Nixon. The young cartoonist was surprisingly skillful, and the jowls and the ski-jump nose are entirely recognizable. Nixon is neatly dressed, solemn in manner—and totally alone.

But although very few felt close to Nixon, most of his class-mates remember him with a respect amounting to awe for his ability and drive, as the letters reproduced in the appendix show. From all this, there emerges at least in rough outline a picture of the kind of boy Nixon was.

There is the genuine Quaker strain, the "very high sense of duty." There is also, as becomes an instinctive conservative, a certain conventionality of outlook. Nixon, unlike many highly intelligent college boys, was never in any way a rebel. On the contrary, he accepted without any hesitation at all the college-boy values of those days (just as Rockefeller did a few years earlier at Dartmouth). To this day, Nixon has never got over his college-boy admiration for football heroes —football is probably the only subject which really interests him, outside of politics. The club song Nixon wrote for the Orthogonians—his only recorded venture in poesy—is almost a parody of the conventional college song:

> All hail the mighty boar,
> Our patron saint is he.
> Our aims forevermore
> In all our deeds must be
> To emulate his might,
> His bravery and his fight.
> Brothers together, we'll travel on and on
> Worthy the name of Orthogonian.

There is also that touch of the ham—a quality most politi-cians possess, but accentuated in his case by the special ham-miness of the southern California atmosphere. There is—especially worth noting—the shrewdness and longheadedness in debate and the brilliant mastery of debating techniques. There is unquestioned ability and first-rate mental equip-ment. And there is something highly unusual in a politician, a withdrawn quality, a lack of easy warmth, and a loneliness of spirit.

There is the urge to manage, to influence, to lead, and an instinct for the means of doing so. And above all, there is the fierce drive, the eagerness to win that took him "offside on almost every play," the hunger for success which made Nixon, as one law-school classmate recalled, "the hardest working man I ever met." This, then, is the basic Nixon. Every one of the characteristics Nixon displayed as a boy is still clearly and visibly present in him. And these characteristics make it possible to understand, if not always to admire, some of the qualities Nixon later displayed as a professional politician.

8

The Case Against

Politics is the most unfair of callings. In no other vocation do professionalism and experience count for so little. The senior partner of an important law firm is not, after all, in danger of being shouldered aside by some upstart who never got a law degree. A poet or a potato-peeler manufacturer is not likely to be given precedence over an experienced financier for the presidency of a bank. And yet the professional politician always hears at his back the winged chariot of the rank amateur, hurrying near.

Twice in the last twenty years—in 1940 and in 1952—the Republican party has turned down the professional and offered its greatest prize to an amateur of the rankest sort. And now the professional, Nixon, hears at his back the winged chariot of the amateur, Rockefeller—although, as this is written, the Rockefeller chariot has a long way to go.

Not that Nelson Rockefeller is an amateur in the sense that
Wendell Willkie was an amateur in 1940, or Dwight Eisenhower in 1952. Unlike them, he has been elected to office, and
to what is usually regarded as the second most important
elective office in the United States. In that office he has han-
dled himself in a decidedly unamateurish manner. Early in
his first year as governor of New York, when State Chairman
Judson Morhouse reported to Rockefeller the bitter opposition in Republican ranks to his proposed tax increase, Rockefeller remarked with a grin: "Tell them I'm just an amateur
in politics, Jud, and maybe they'll go easy on me." Morhouse
replied: "I'll tell them that, Nelson, but I don't know how I
can keep my face straight." All present guffawed knowingly.

There was nothing amateurish about the way Rockefeller
went about getting the Republican gubernatorial nomination
in 1958, nor about his campaign against Averell Harriman,
which was calculated in a most professional manner to cut
heavily into the normal Democratic majority in New York
City. And there is nothing amateurish either about the way
in which Rockefeller, as this is written, is preparing to challenge Nixon. It has been cynically remarked that only one
episode in Rockefeller's presidential candidacy was the result
of pure chance—his son's fortuitous marriage to the Nor-
wegian Cinderella, Miss Rasmussen. Everything else was
planned in advance with the most consummate attention to
detail. If the challenge to Nixon is never issued—on this point
the reader is better able to judge than the writer—it will be
for one reason only. It will be because a highly professional
assessment of the real political situation has led Rockefeller to the conclusion that Nixon cannot be beaten for the
nomination.

And yet Rockefeller is not a professional politician, all the
same, in the sense that Nixon is a professional politician. He
has held elective office only since January 1959—far too
briefly to attain the professional aura. Unlike the true pro-

fessional, he has decidedly never had to depend on politics for his daily bread, nor has politics been, all his adult life, his chief *raison d'être,* as it has been Nixon's reason for being.

Any attempt to summarize the case against Rockefeller side by side with the case against Nixon suggests why politics is the only profession in which it is a positive advantage not to be a professional. The case against Rockefeller is vague, fuzzy, and largely a matter of personal opinion or prejudice. The case against Nixon is detailed, specific, and, to at least some intelligent and fair-minded people, convincing.

It is not very hard, to be sure, to find people who know Rockefeller and who believe that he would make a disastrous President. One of those who came to know him and dislike him intensely in the wartime days, and who is now a re- spected back-room boy in Democratic affairs, has said flatly that he would far prefer Nixon to Rockefeller as President, if there had to be a choice. "You know how I feel about Nixon," he says, "but at least with him we'd know where we stood, and you never know where you stand with Rocke- feller. I'd rather 'bear those ills we have than fly to others that we know not of.'"

Here is an anti-Rockefellerite who saw Rockefeller in ac- tion in Eisenhower's Washington: "Because Nelson's never had to worry about money, he has no real idea of its value. And he's just as extravagant with people as he is with money. He had something like eighty people working for him in that cold-war adviser's job—Bill Jackson, who succeeded him, found there wasn't enough work for half a dozen. The budget and the bureaucracy would both get out of hand if he ever became President."

Even some of those who know him well and admire him have their private doubts about a Rockefeller presidency. "Nelson has only one real fault, but it's a serious one," says one friend. "He has no real critical faculty. I've seen him rubbing his hands with enthusiasm over half a dozen wild-eyed schemes. In the White House, that could be a dangerous business."

Another, and closer, friend has this to say: "Nelson's one great weakness is that, because of his circumstances, he has never known *real* pain, *real* suffering, *real* defeat. As a result, his world is an unreal world, a lopsided world. He is the embodiment of the great American illusion that all problems are soluble, that if you devote enough brain power and enough money to a problem, you always come up with the answer. He does not realize that there are some problems which have no answer, and that worries me when I think he might be President."

There may be some truth in all these opinions, even the harshest. But they are opinions, nothing more, and it is easy to unearth hostile opinions of any man in public life. It is not possible to point to something Rockefeller has done or said which a man who aspires to the awful power of the presidency ought not to have done or said. It is entirely possible to point to things that Nixon has said (not done) which a man who aspires to the presidency ought not to have said.

Part of the case against Nixon is, quite simply, untrue. For example, there is the story that in his 1946 campaign against Jerry Voorhis, an anonymous telephone-call drive was organized by Nixon. According to the story, vast numbers of voters answered the telephone and heard: "This is a friend of yours. I just wanted you to know that Jerry Voorhis is a Communist." The caller would then hang up immediately.

The story, which has also been told about Nixon's campaign against Helen Gahagan Douglas, is devoutly believed by many intelligent people. It has been frequently repeated in print—for example, in the *Democratic Fact Book* in 1956. But it is not true. Murray Chotiner once explained to me why it was not true. To have any appreciable effect on the outcome of an election in a large congressional district, Chotiner pointed out calmly, such a drive would have to be highly organized, with a large work force daily telephoning thousands of names. It would be impossible to keep secret an operation organized on such a basis. Even if it were possible, he said in effect, the operation would be self-defeating in the end—sooner or later one of those involved would turn on the candidate and would be willing to describe the whole operation in print, and if necessary under oath. This would ruin the candidate politically, and incidentally his political manager. For such practical reasons, no political manager in his senses would organize such an operation.

If only because it was based on such highly practical considerations, the explanation seemed to me wholly convincing. No doubt some people got anonymous telephone calls.[1] Such calls are a regular feature of any heated political situation. But if the story about Nixon's anonymous telephone drive were true, it would be easy to prove, and a lot of powerful people would give their eyeteeth to prove it. No real evidence to support it has ever been produced.

Among other flatly untrue stories about Nixon is the charge that "the slush fund enabled Nixon to make the down payment on his Washington home"—this appeared in *The Nixon Record* published by the Democratic National Committee in 1956. What really made it possible for Nixon to make the down payment on his house was his remarkable proficiency as a poker player. In the fund speech Nixon said, "My service record was not particularly unusual—I was just there when the bombs were falling." The statement was accurate enough, although, since Nixon had a non-combat job far from the battle lines, there presumably were not many bombs.[2] All the same, Nixon's war career was unusual in one way. He

---

[1] *When my younger brother John Alsop persuaded a Republican town caucus in Avon, Connecticut, unanimously to condemn Senator Joseph McCarthy in 1953, he got anonymous calls accusing him of being a Communist for some time thereafter.*

[2] *Of all the current crop of candidates, the only genuine war hero is Senator Kennedy.*

became an unusually proficient poker player, and as a result he came back from the wars with a useful nest egg—about $10,000, according to the report of one Nixon intimate. The nest egg has provided him with the wherewithal for such personal capital expenditures as the down payment on his house.

There are other items in the case against Nixon which are unquestionably true, but which are not really as damning as they are supposed to be (or at least they do not seem so to me). For example, there is the famous "pink sheet," printed on orders from Murray Chotiner in the 1950 campaign for the Senate, in which Helen Gahagan Douglas's voting record was compared with that of the pro-Communist Representative Vito Marcantonio. Certainly this was hardly an admirable political technique. But it is true that Mrs. Douglas started the game of "you're another" by comparing Nixon's voting record on Korean aid to Marcantonio's. It is also true that Mrs. Douglas was in fact vulnerable on certain issues, like her vote against Greek-Turkish aid.

But the real reason I have never been able to get very excited about the pink sheet is that the idea was first thought up by none other than my brother and myself. Early in the summer of 1950 we wrote a column, called "The Republican Party Line," which achieved a certain réclame at the time. The column compared the voting records of such Republican isolationists as Senators Taft, Wherry, and Kem, on foreign and defense issues, with the record of Marcantonio on the same issues. We noted that Taft scored an eighty-five per cent, and Wherry and Kem scored one hundred per cent. As I wrote to the Louisville *Courier-Journal,* which had accused me in an editorial of softness toward Nixon, "I do not recall any violent outcry from liberals when that piece was published."

All this is not meant to suggest that Nixon's campaigns in 1946 and 1950 were "elevated democratic dialogues," to borrow a Stevensonian phrase. They were very rough campaigns indeed, and in some ways they were worse than rough. But the roughness was on both sides, especially in the 1950 campaign, as Earl Mazo's factual and heavily documented account of that campaign makes clear. And in both campaigns the fact is that Nixon simply adopted the basic Republican line, with variations of his own. In 1946 Republicans all over the country were running, like Nixon, against the meat shortage and the CIO-PAC. In 1950, again like Nixon, Republicans all over the country were running against communism and corruption (Nixon, unlike many other Republicans, did not run against the Korean War).

It is in this sense that the fact that Nixon has been a professional politician since 1946 is like an albatross around his neck—and Nelson Rockefeller, a non-professional, wears no such albatross. A lot of the things that the Republican professionals all over the country were saying in 1946 or 1950 or 1952 were silly, or extreme, or both. But in retrospect they seem even sillier and more extreme. Nixon's position is further compromised by the fact that, before he became Vice-President, he served in the House and Senate. A member of Congress must cast dozens of votes which inevitably alienate large voting groups, which is one reason why only one sitting member of Congress has been nominated and elected President in all our history, the disastrous Warren G. Harding.

"I know the Democrats will try to picture me as an extremist," Nixon has said, "but you can't go on hashing up the distant past indefinitely." You can go on hashing up the distant past for a good long time, though—some Republicans are still running against Yalta, and some Democrats are still running against Herbert Hoover. And Nixon's past provides a rich gold mine of direct quotations calculated to alienate and embitter almost all Democrats and a great many independents. Partly because he has never run for office as a professional party-line Republican—and partly also because,

unlike Nixon, he is not an instinctively partisan man—Rockefeller's past provides no such gold mine.

But the case against Nixon by no means rests entirely on
the fact that he is and has long been a professional, party-line
Republican. For, at least until 1954, Nixon displayed what
sometimes seems almost a compulsion to use specious and
sleazy debating tricks in order to "make the worse appear
the better reason."

Consider a few of these debating tricks. There is the juxta-
position of words, as when Nixon, in 1952, in the course of
accusing Truman and Stevenson of tolerating Communists
in the government, called them "traitors to the high principles of the Democratic party." In the context of those days
when McCarthy rode high, the words "traitor" and "democratic party" were the words that remained in his hearers'
minds.

There is the use of the undeniable statement with a false
implication. An example from the fund speech: "Every penny
of it was used to pay for political expenses that I did not
think should be charged to the taxpayers of the United
States." In fact, the purpose of the fund was to meet expenses
which *could not* be charged to the taxpayers of the United
States.

There is the trick of the coupling of categories, as in the
1954 campaign statement: "We have driven the Communists,
the fellow travellers, and the security risks out of government
by thousands." It is true that several thousand so-called
"security risks" were dropped in the early Eisenhower years
to appease McCarthy. But Nixon failed to point out that the
vast majority of these people were fired for reasons having
nothing to do with subversion, that many of them were hired
initially by the Eisenhower administration itself, and that
the total included not a single known Communist. Thus
again, the implication of what he said was false.

The year 1954 was a bad year for Nixon. In that year, Nixon

came closest to justifying Walter Lippmann's description of him as a "ruthless partisan . . . (who) does not have within his conscience those scruples which the country has the right to expect in the President of the United States." Two statements Nixon made in 1954 best sum up the case against Nixon.

In a speech in Los Angeles, Nixon quoted Adlai Stevenson as saying that "while the American economy has been shrinking, the Soviet economy has been growing fast." On that basis he accused Stevenson of being "guilty without being aware that he was doing so of spreading pro-Communist propaganda." Again there is the old debater's trick, in the phrase "without being aware that he was doing so," which simultaneously suggests that the speaker is being fairminded and that his victim is too stupid to know what he is doing. It was a disgraceful thing to say, the more so because Nixon, who does his homework, must have known that Stevenson's warnings were fully justified. In the spring of 1958, indeed, in an admirable speech, Nixon warned of the deadly challenge implicit in the extraordinarily rapid growth of the Soviet economy. He was thus guilty, by his own definition, of "spreading pro-Communist propaganda."

But if there is any one sentence which best sums up the case against Nixon it is the famous aside in a 1954 telecast defending the Eisenhower-Dulles foreign policies. Nixon looked up from his script and asked, as though on the spur of the moment: "And incidentally, in mentioning Secretary Dulles, isn't it wonderful finally to have a Secretary of State who isn't taken in by the Communists?"

Nixon didn't say that Dean G. Acheson and George Marshall were "taken in by the Communists." But he very clearly implied it, and the implication is grossly misleading. To make his implication, Nixon made use of both an essentially specious "Communist issue" and a sleazy debater's trick, the rhetorical question. He asked his rhetorical question, more-

over, not when he was a young congressman engaged in what
he has called a "rocking, socking campaign," but when he
had already been Vice-President of the United States for two
years. Even better than the disgraceful statement about Stevenson, in short, that rhetorical question explains why, to
some reasonable and fair-minded people, the case against
Nixon is a convincing case.

To understand all is not necessarily to forgive all. Even so,
it is worth trying to understand why Nixon was, even as late
as 1954, the kind of politician who could ask that rhetorical
question. And to one familiar with Nixon's early history, understanding is not really so very difficult.

There were the circumstances to which he was born. There
was the Irish ancestry, and Nixon's inborn "instinct to strike
back." There were the parents who wanted him to be "good,
not just at one thing, but at everything"—and especially the
cantankerous, ulcer-ridden father, urging him to win at all
costs. And there were also Nixon's years as a champion college debater, years which formed his speaking style. The object of college debating, after all, is quite simply to win the
debate, just as it is the object of college football to win the
game. The debate is won by scoring points off the opposition,
using whatever debating techniques come to hand. The
championship debater need not, and indeed should not, concern himself with the merits of the issues, since he must be
prepared to defend either side.

It may seem farfetched to try to explain Nixon the politician in terms of Nixon the champion boy debater of southern
California. Yet I am convinced that Nixon's training as a
debater really is an important part of the explanation. Remember that Nixon's first great triumphs centered around
debating—debating made him a big man on the Whittier
campus, and debating got his name and picture in the august
Los Angeles *Times*. In the course of my reporting I have
collected a vast anti-Nixon dossier. Ninety-eight per cent of

the dossier consists of examples of tricky debating techniques like those cited above. And in case after case it seems almost inconceivable that Nixon's use of such techniques had any important impact on the voting. He used them, one suspects, simply because he was trained in their use.

At any rate, at least half the case against Nixon rests on the fact that even until 1954 he seemed to see nothing wrong in using such debating tricks in his public speeches. But that is not the whole case against Nixon. The other half of the case against Nixon is that, at least until 1954, he was the sort of politician who saw winning elections as the first, and in a sense the only, function of a politician.

The way Nixon became a politician is as important as the circumstances to which he was born, in any attempt to understand why he became the kind of politician he did become. In 1945 Nixon was renegotiating Navy contracts in Baltimore and, like thousands of other veterans, worrying unhappily about his future, when he got a telegram from Herbert Perry, a family friend who managed the Whittier branch of the Bank of America. Perry suggested that Nixon might like to come back to Whittier to address a Republican committee which was fruitlessly searching for a candidate to oppose the well-entrenched Jerry Voorhis. Nixon accepted the unexpected invitation, and his earnest clichés convinced the committee members that he was their man. So the Nixon political career was launched.

Nixon became a politician, in short, more because it seemed a good idea at the time than because of any profound political convictions. Having thus entered politics more or less by accident, one suspects that at first he thought of a political career much as another young veteran back from the wars might think of advertising, or meat packing, or bond selling—as a way to make a living and get ahead. In politics, obviously, you don't get ahead unless you get elected—and then re-elected. And Nixon soon acquired a political mentor

in the person of the astute Murray Chotiner, that expert in
the art of winning elections at all costs and by any means.
The way to win is to beat your opponent, and one way to
beat your opponent is to develop a fine instinct for his weak-
est point, his Achilles' heel, his political jugular vein.

There is no doubt that Nixon became adept at finding the
opposition's political jugular, and often the jugular was the
"Communist issue." Often enough, in turn, the "Communist
issue" was essentially specious, a debating trick, as in that
famous rhetorical question. And yet, in all fairness, Nixon's
experience in the Hiss case ought to be considered in any
rational attempt to weigh the case against Nixon.

Before the Hiss case, Nixon's only unusual experience in
Congress had been his service on the Herter committee on
foreign aid, which persuaded Nixon that it was wholly in
this country's interest to make a serious effort to shore up
the free world. (He has acted and voted consistently on that
conviction ever since.) But it was the Hiss case that first
made Nixon's face visible in the faceless mass in the House.
Nixon was just another congressman until 1948, when Alger
Hiss came along—indeed, he largely owes his present emi-
nence to his fellow Quaker, Hiss.

This is not the place to rehash the old, complex, tragic
story of Alger Hiss. But although there are still odd mysteries
clinging to the story, few fair-minded persons who have read
the record have any serious doubt that Hiss was guilty. And
there is equally little serious doubt that Nixon, on the whole,
behaved intelligently and responsibly, and that, if it had not
been for his stubborn efforts, Hiss in all likelihood would not
have been brought to justice. At any rate, the Hiss case was
Nixon's first really important political experience. In human
terms, it thus seems natural enough that Nixon should develop something of an obsession about communism. And
in the McCarthy era, plenty of politicians suddenly devel-

oped an obsession about communism with far less excuse for doing so.

Nixon's relationship with McCarthy, as well as his often specious political use of the "Communist issue," is usually cited as part of the case against Nixon. And it is true that Nixon never took a stand against McCarthy until the Wisconsin demagogue had been politically destroyed. But it is worth recalling, again in all fairness, that with a handful of honorable exceptions, every Republican politician was in the early days either gleefully pro-McCarthy or carefully noncommittal; that the entire Eisenhower administration quivered with collective fear at mention of the dreaded McCarthy name; and that not more than one Democrat out of five had dared to speak out against the Great Inquisitor.

Nixon's actual role in the early McCarthy days was to act as the Eisenhower administration's ambassador to McCarthy, and for a time, as in the matter of the confirmation of Charles E. Bohlen, he performed rather usefully in that role. In any case, if Nixon is to be condemned because he failed to fight McCarthy, a very large number of politicians in both parties should beware of casting the first stone.

All this is not to suggest that there is no case against Nixon. The case against Nixon is real, and it can be simply summarized. Until 1954, Nixon was the sort of politician who regarded winning elections as a politician's first and most important function, and who was willing to use to that end the tricky debating techniques he had learned as a boy. A President who regarded winning elections as his first function, and who was willing to use sleazy debating tricks to that end, would be a disastrous President. Therefore, it is important to ask whether Nixon is still the same sort of politician he once was.

Nixon's numerous enemies scoff at the notion that Nixon has changed in any way. To elicit howls of derision where two or three Democrats are gathered together in one place,

it is only necessary to utter the phrase, "the new Nixon." And
in one sense the howls of derision are justified. There are
ways in which men do not change. A boy's intelligence quotient at the age of nine will be about the same when he is
forty-five. A born fool or a born coward will so remain. As
the Bible warns, a man cannot "by taking thought . . . add
one cubit unto his stature."

Yet time and experience do change a man, not in his inner
nature but rather as saline deposits change the size and shape
of a barnacle exposed to the sea. It is silly to suppose that a
man of Nixon's intelligence and capacity to learn has been
in no way affected by the extraordinary experiences through
which he has passed.

And one fact can be proved on the record. In his style as a
politician, if not in his character as a human being, Nixon
has changed. The change started in 1954. For after 1954 the
anti-Nixon dossier suddenly dwindles away into almost nothing at all. Indeed, there are only two items worth mentioning.
One was his reference in 1956 to Chief Justice Earl Warren
as a "great Republican Chief Justice." This was no doubt very
naughty, although the notion that Supreme Court justices
become political eunuchs at the moment of their appointment
is rather sillier than most of our national myths.

The other major item in the post-1954 dossier consists of
Nixon's reaction to a New York *Times* story in 1958. The
story was to the effect that letters to the State Department
were running four to one against the Administration's firm
stand in the Quemoy-Matsu crisis. When Nixon read the
story, he issued an angry statement. The main point of the
statement was Nixon's attack on "the apparent assumption
that . . . the weight of the mail rather than the weight of
the evidence should be the controlling factor in determining
American foreign policy." In this respect, surely, Nixon was
eternally right. But he also professed to discern a "patent

and deliberate effort of a State Department subordinate to undercut the Secretary of State and sabotage his policy."

This statement caused many ghosts which had long been laid to walk again. For here, suddenly, was "the old Nixon," seeing "deliberate sabotage" in the State Department where there was nothing more than enterprising reporting; the old Nixon who interpreted complex situations in terms of individual villains. "Oh dear," one of Nixon's admirers sighed on that occasion, "why does Dick always have to go too far?"

And yet, the fact is that, since 1954, Nixon has very rarely gone too far, although the provocation has often been great. In 1956, for example, Adlai Stevenson's campaign strategists quite frankly hoped to drive Nixon to extremes by brutal attacks on his integrity and past record. To their profound disappointment, Nixon, who was of course quite aware of what they were up to, built his campaign around the ticket's "positive" asset—the President's personal popularity. He "finessed," to use his own word, the attacks on him, as he now advises younger politicians to do. In the 1958 non-presidential election, there were those who professed to see "the old Nixon" in some of Nixon's more partisan statements. In fact, Nixon said no more than what party-line Republicans were saying everywhere in the country.

The change in Nixon's political style since 1954 is, in short, obvious and on the record. It may be possible to pinpoint the moment when he decided to change his style.

In his early years in Washington, especially during the Hiss case era, Nixon was extremely sensitive to criticism. When criticized, he was likely to fly into a Black Irish temper. (I have never seen him angry, but his temper is said to be very violent on the rare occasions when he loses control of it.) In the last several years, however, Nixon has come to regard criticism as a useful means of improving the public performance of Richard Nixon, and he is oddly dispassionate about it. From certain friends, Nixon nowadays asks for candid criticism.

One of these friends is Philip Watts, an able banker and former State Department official, whom Nixon first met when Watts was secretary of the Herter committee. Nixon's friends and associates are apt to be shrewdly practical men with a talent for *realpolitik*, but Watts is quite different. He is idealistic to the point of naïveté, and one suspects that Nixon has quite consciously used him as a sort of perambulating conscience, a counterweight to his more practical advisers. In the McCarthy era, Watts was the only really passionate anti-McCarthyite who was close to Nixon. The strong anti-McCarthy line Watts took with Nixon may have helped prevent Nixon from becoming more closely identified with McCarthy than he did become.

It is at least possible that Watts had an important influence on Nixon's post-McCarthy career. When Nixon asked his famous rhetorical question, Watts heard the telecast, and at nine-thirty the next morning he was in Nixon's office asking to see the Vice-President. At eleven he was shown into the Nixon inner sanctum. He wasted no time in telling Nixon what he thought of his remark. The implications of Nixon's aside were wholly specious, he said—he had worked for Dean Acheson, and it was disgraceful to imply that Acheson had been "taken in by the Communists." Moreover, if Nixon wanted the respect of honorable men, he should promptly abandon his habit of making his points by indirection, especially by the sly debater's trick of the rhetorical question.

"I expected to be thrown bodily out of the office," Watts recalls. For a time, Nixon had obvious difficulty in controlling his temper. But both men calmed down in the end, and they talked for a long time, with Nixon citing the Hiss case to defend the implications of his question, while Watts begged him, as a friend, to drop his technique of scoring points off the opposition by indirection. "He never admitted for a moment that he was wrong," Watts recalls, "but I think he thought about what I said."

Whether or not the talk with Watts had anything to do with it, the change in Nixon's political style since 1954 has been quite obvious to anyone not blinded by bitterness toward him. For the cynical, there is an easy explanation to hand. In 1954, Nixon did not want to be President—or at least he did not think he had any chance to be President. He had seriously promised Pat Nixon that he would never run for office again. (He still owes his friend James Bassett ten dollars, for in 1954 Bassett bet him that he *would* run again.) By 1956 and thereafter, Nixon did want to be President. He wanted to be President very much, and he knew that he had a chance, perhaps a good chance, to become President. But he also knew—for he is anything but a fool—that a reputation as an extremist and partisan would sharply reduce that chance. Hence his change of political style.

A man's motives are always mixed, and no doubt it is true that Nixon changed his political style after 1954 in part for purely practical political reasons. But does the change go deeper than that?

The reader is in just about as good a position to answer that question as the writer, for of course any answer is sheer guesswork, a matter of instinct. It may be that those who instinctively distrust Nixon are right in supposing that he has simply put on another mask, more suited to his presidential ambitions than the mask of the pre-1954 Nixon. At least there is no way to prove that they are wrong. But my guess, for what it is worth, is that they are wrong, nevertheless.

Nixon unquestionably wants very much to be President. But it seems to me that he also wants very much to be a good President. To suppose otherwise of the product of the prim Quaker household, whose parents spurred him on to be "good at everything," to suppose that Nixon wants to be President out of a cynical love of power and for no other reason, is to suppose that Nixon is some sort of monster, which he is not. It is because he not only wants to be President but also wants to be a good President that Nixon has worked harder than any Vice-President in history at his job.

Moreover, the evidence suggests that his attitude toward the presidency has changed. To any Vice-President, the thought must sometimes occur that he might wake up President tomorrow. As long as the President is in rude health, the thought is casual and fleeting, as distant and unreal as the thought of a man's own death. But the President's heart attack in September 1955 certainly made the thought that he might become President real, and vivid, and immediate, to Nixon. Since then, Nixon has not only thought with his brain that he might succeed to the presidency—he has known it in his heart. The magnifying and transforming effect of the presidential office has often been noted. Even at one remove, the office has had an effect on Nixon.

When he became Vice-President in 1952, and for some time thereafter, Nixon thought of the presidency, one suspects, primarily as the first prize in the political game. He thought of the office, perhaps, rather as an ambitious young Detroit executive might think of the presidency of General Motors, as ambition's final crown. But there is a lot more to the presidency than simply reaching the top of the heap, and it seems silly to suppose that Nixon, a highly intelligent and perceptive man, still regards the presidency simply as the first prize in politics, after so many years of intimate exposure to the terrible responsibilities of that office. One of those responsibilities is to be right on the basic life-and-death issues, even when it is politically unwise to be right, and Nixon, in recent years, has been right rather often.

Nixon instantly recognized and publicly acknowledged the real significance of the Soviet Sputniks when other Administration officials were trying to laugh it off with weak jokes. Both in the pre-Sputnik and post-Sputnik era, Nixon strongly opposed the policy of defense cutback and slow-down—that kind of economy, he warned, might be good politics in the short run, but it would be bad politics in the long run. When the President overruled him on the issue, he supported the President, to be sure—he felt that, as Vice-President, he had no alternative, and perhaps he was right. At least he understood the nature of the threat inherent in the growing Soviet preponderance of power. Nixon has also loudly and consistently advocated an adequate foreign-aid program. Indeed, in Nelson Rockefeller's struggle with the Four H Club on this issue he was Rockefeller's strongest, and almost his only, ally. Since almost all politicians agree that foreign aid is political poison, it is difficult even for the cynical to detect the political motivation in Nixon's stand on the issue.

It is true that a man cannot, by taking thought, add a cubit to his stature, or increase his intelligence quotient, or substitute courage for cowardice in his character. But we do grow up, and the growing-up process does not necessarily end when we reach our prescribed height. Few men in their forties or fifties would defend everything they said or did in their twenties and thirties. Nixon's job has provided as good a medium of forced growth as there is, short of the presidency itself. Perhaps the best evidence that he has grown was provided by his famous tour of the Soviet Union and Poland in the summer of 1959.

It would be excessively naïve to suggest that the trip was not in part politically motivated, of course. Nixon's aides were candidly rueful, indeed, that the trip had to be almost a year in advance of the Republican convention—the impact would have been far greater if the convention had assembled with Nixon's triumph still fresh in the delegates' minds. But just because the political implications of Nixon's tour were so obvious, there were sensible people who feared that Nixon would again "go too far," by making grandstand plays for the

huge Polish-American voting bloc, for example. Instead, even
his critics were impressed by his performance. It was indeed
a remarkable performance, by a mature and responsible politician. It is hard to imagine the Nixon of ten years ago per-
forming in the same way.

What kind of President, then, might Nixon be? And what
kind of President might Rockefeller be?

These questions are, of course, inherently unanswerable,
since there are too many imponderables involved. But it is
possible to make at least a sensible guess at the answers from
what we know about the two men. An attempt at such a guess
will be made in the final chapter of this book.

9

What Kind of President?

The men around a President tell a great deal about the sort of President he is. Eisenhower's conservatism, in some ways more marked than Taft's ever was, his initial political naïveté, and his military man's respect for the successful money-maker were characteristics accurately reflected in the first Eisenhower cabinet, described at the time as consisting of "nine millionaires and a plumber." Truman's oddly schizophrenic approach to the presidency was reflected with equal accuracy by the men around him. Those who dealt solely with domestic matters were, for the most part, second or third raters, whereas on the foreign and defense-policy fronts Truman recruited, with the single exception of Louis Johnson, as able a group of men as Washington has seen in modern times.

It would be silly, of course, to try to identify in advance

the men a President Rockefeller or a President Nixon might appoint to high office. But it is possible to identify the men who are close to Rockefeller and Nixon now, and who will presumably remain close to them. In both cases, the men around them tell a good deal about the kind of President Nixon or Rockefeller might become.

Rockefeller is the sort of man who attracts a vast entourage. Ever since he was in his twenties he has been surrounded by a princely retinue of "Rockefeller men, first, last, and all the time." The pecking order within the entourage is established by the individual's personal relations with Rockefeller and access to him. The pecking order is in a constant state of flux, with those on the outer fringes suddenly moving toward the center, and vice versa.

Indeed, working for Rockefeller is an ulcer-generating experience, by all accounts, despite his solicitude for the personal well-being of his dependents. Like Franklin Roosevelt, Rockefeller has a habit of appointing two men to do the same job, or overlapping jobs, and then sitting back, with an air of bland unconcern, to see which of the two fighting cocks he has thrown into the ring comes out on top. Again, one suspects that Rockefeller quite consciously emulates the peculiar administrative methods of Roosevelt, for the instability of the pecking order among the men around him was one of the main sources of Roosevelt's control of the bureaucracy. In a Rockefeller administration, the executive branch of the government would doubtless present as bloodily exciting a spectacle as in Roosevelt's day. There are those who maintain that the blood and excitement are essential to achievement and are thus far more valuable than any amount of neat and orderly administration.

Despite the instability of the Rockefeller pecking order, there has been for a good many years a rather stable Inner Circle—as the small group of people who are really close to Rockefeller are called in almost audible capitals by lesser members of the entourage. Wallace Harrison, architect for Rockefeller Center, the man who accompanied Rockefeller on that stormy voyage to Seal Harbor, is perhaps the leading member of the Inner Circle. Most people consider Harrison Rockefeller's closest personal friend. He is a highly intelligent man, humorous, scholarly, articulate, of a rather philosophical turn of mind, a bit older than Rockefeller, and, on superficial acquaintance at least, rather surprising in the role of Rockefeller's best friend. Another member of the Inner Circle is John Lockwood, the able Rockefeller lawyer and chief man of business, who is the closest thing to a "no-man" in the Rockefeller entourage. It is unlikely that Rockefeller would appoint either man to high office. But they would be important figures in a Rockefeller administration, all the same, for Rockefeller would continue to consult them privately, as he has done for two decades or more.

The third member of the Inner Circle is Frank Jamieson, a former Democrat who is public relations adviser to the Rockefeller family. Rockefeller has three press agents at the present writing, all three, oddly enough, ex-Democrats. As this multiplicity of public relations experts suggests, Rockefeller has an excessive respect for the dubious arts of press agentry, just as he has for the pseudo science of public-opinion polling.

His excessive respect for press agentry may explain in part why he has had his troubles with the press, both in Washington, where he never got a really good press, and in Albany, where the press staged a brief "revolt" shortly after he became governor. His worst mistakes occurred in August 1959, when he attended the Governors' Conference in Puerto Rico. He invited a carefully selected group of reporters to talk with him on a "no direct quotation or attribution" basis. This was mistake number one—since he invited only about half the reporters present, the uninvited half were furious. He then committed mistake number two when he told the group that he would make up his mind whether or not to become an active

candidate on the basis of his and Nixon's comparative standing in the polls, probably in November.

This was mistake number two, and a bad one. It invited
comparison between his standing in the polls and Nixon's at
a time when Nixon's Russian triumph would still be fresh in
people's minds and when Nixon might very well stand higher
than Rockefeller. Worse, it seemed to imply that Rockefeller
was ready to turn over the whole democratic political process to Dr. Gallup and his colleagues. Then, after coming
back, and after conferring with Thomas E. Dewey, Rockefeller called another press conference. Instead of saying that
he had been misunderstood, the classic formula in such circumstances, he denied saying what he had said, thus making
liars out of a powerful group of respected newspapermen.
This was his third mistake, and probably his worst.

If Frank Jamieson had not been seriously ill, Rockefeller
might not have made these egregious errors. But aside from
this unhappy episode, Rockefeller has been learning rather
rapidly how to handle the press, both in press conferences,
where he has displayed that "facility essential to the politician" which Nixon ascribed to Frol Kozlov, and in the often
more important private contacts. He appears to have learned
the essential lesson—that a really important political figure
can no more delegate responsibility for his relations with the
press than a man can delegate responsibility for his relations
with his wife.

The job of a press agent is, or ought to be, essentially a
technical job, but within those limits it is an important job.
Jamieson is easily the ablest of the Rockefeller public relations men, and if he recovers from his illness and if Rockefeller reaches the White House, Jamieson is likely to be as
important a figure in a Rockefeller administration as James
Hagerty has been in the Eisenhower administration.

The fourth member of the Inner Circle is Louise Boyer,
Rockefeller's coolly capable confidential secretary. In an un-

8

obtrusive way, she would also be a key figure in a Rockefeller administration, for Rockefeller depends heavily on her. That completes the list of the true Inner Circle. Worth noting is the fact that three of the four Inner Circle-ites are employed in the vast family suite in Rockefeller Center, and although Wallace Harrison is not an employee of the Rockefellers, they are his most important clients.

About the only discoverable Rockefeller intimate who has no connection with the Rockefeller interests is Deputy Secretary of Defense Thomas Gates (who may be Secretary of Defense when this book is published). The two men were brought together by their wives, who are fellow Philadelphians and close friends and who share an interest in nursing. Gates and Rockefeller jointly own a summer shack on Shingle Island, a spot of land off the Maine coast, for which they paid three hundred dollars before the war. Occasionally the two families spend a rugged weekend together on Shingle Island. But even Gates is by no means as close to Rockefeller as the members of the true Inner Circle.

There are a number of candidate members of the Inner Circle, who would presumably play a significant part in a Rockefeller administration. There is Roswell Perkins, a highly intelligent young lawyer who has worked for Rockefeller both in Washington and Albany. There is William Ronan, Rockefeller's able appointments secretary and man of all work in Albany. There is the budget director, Norman Hurd, the man who finally persuaded Rockefeller that he had no choice but to raise taxes (and thereby, perhaps, knocked his boss out of the presidential race). But the really important apprentice members of the Inner Circle are Republican National Committeeman George Hinman and State Chairman Judson Morhouse.

The key role played by Morhouse in Rockefeller's preconvention bid for the New York gubernatorial nomination has already been mentioned. As the supposedly neutral state

chairman he bet his political shirt on Rockefeller. His chief
role was to persuade the upstate leaders to hold off, while the
Rockefeller candidacy was gaining steam. He would show the
upstate delegate-owners Rockefeller-subsidized polls showing Rockefeller running ahead of Leonard Hall and the other
potential candidates. "You've got nothing to lose by waiting,"
Morhouse told them all. "Wait till you see this Rockefeller
before you commit yourself." Rockefeller would duly appear,
turn on the famous charm, and "the guys would swoon."

If Rockefeller had lost either the nomination or the election,
Morhouse would have been a very dead politician. But his
long-shot bet paid off, and if the long-shot bet he is now making on Rockefeller for President also pays off, he will be one
of the country's biggest political movers and shakers. Morhouse is an ebullient redhead with an engaging candor and
an amusing turn of speech—the sort of politician you might
expect to make a long-shot political bet. George Hinman, an
upstater who inherited a Bull Moose political background,
and who also bet early on Rockefeller, is a highly intelligent
man, and he is, one suspects, a considerably wilier operator
than Morhouse. Together, Morhouse and Hinman make up
a sort of composite Jim Farley, with Morhouse cast in the role
of contact man and front-room boy, and Hinman as the back-
room boy and chief political strategist. The combination is a
formidable one.

There are others, who are not in Nelson Rockefeller's retinue, who are not his men, but who will strongly influence his
course. There are his brothers, for example, all able men in
their way. The Rockefeller family is very close-knit, and the
family will certainly be consulted if Nelson ever gets to the
White House. There are also the men, a rather amorphous
group, mostly with large financial interests and mostly from
New York City, who always have a lot to say at Republican
conventions. Rockefeller has close contacts in this group. His
uncle Winthrop Aldrich, for example, former Ambassador to

Britain and former president of the Chase bank, is a member of the group, and he has backed the winning candidate for the nomination at every Republican convention since 1936.

Rockefeller's personal and financial relationships with what is incorrectly called "the Wall Street crowd" by no means assure him the nomination. He will be backed by the New York group only if it is the consensus of expert opinion that he can win and that Nixon cannot, and on that point much attention will be paid to the views of Thomas E. Dewey. If both appear to have about an equal chance of winning, it will certainly be Nixon. There is no doubt at all on that point. For the New Yorkers do not have the same reasons for opposing Nixon as they had for opposing Taft—Nixon, for example, is no isolationist—and Rockefeller could be nominated only after a bruising party fight which all concerned wish to avoid if the price for avoiding it is not the seemingly certain loss of the White House to the Democrats.

Rockefeller's New York connections have another meaning, however. Painful as it is for those from other parts to admit it, New York's financial and legal circles provide incomparably the country's greatest reservoir of ability. Moreover, there seems to be a well-established rule that whereas such provincial industrial managers as Charles Wilson and George Humphrey find it almost impossible to shake their acquired managerial prejudices and take a truly national view, the products of Wall Street and environs make remarkably effective civil servants. The names of Forrestal, Lovett, Harriman, McCloy, Nitze, Finletter, Dillon come to mind—there are many others. For obvious reasons, if he became President, Rockefeller would certainly not staff the higher reaches of his Administration predominantly with New York financial or legal luminaries. Yet no presidential candidate in American political history has had closer personal and business ties with the ablest of such men, and it seems safe to predict that

Rockefeller, as President, would tap to the fullest possible extent New York's vast reservoir of ability.

One thing is completely safe to predict about a Rockefeller presidency. Rockefeller would dominate the executive branch absolutely. Every important post would be filled with a "Rockefeller man first, last, and all the time." And although it is true that "Nelson doesn't expect you to be a yes-man," it is also true that Rockefeller has no no-men, with the possible exception of John Lockwood, around him. One of those who has worked for him for a long time explains Rockefeller's attitude toward subordinates as follows:

"Say Nelson had decided there was something that ought to be done, like preserving the state's timber reserves—he's always been hot for conservation, like the two Roosevelts. Well, if he asked for your advice on a plan for conserving timber, he wouldn't mind a bit if you said, 'I think that's a lousy way to do it—here's a better way to do it.' But if you said you thought his objective was wrong, that the state government had no business preserving timber, and that he ought to give up the whole idea, then you'd be out on your ear. See the difference?"

Rockefeller, in short, would certainly demand, and get, "positive loyalty" from the executive branch. As for the other main branch of the American government, the only way to judge how he would deal with Congress is to examine his way of dealing with the New York State Legislature. As we have seen, as a believer in what his grandfather called "method," Rockefeller had carefully prepared himself in advance with his 134 "studies," which dealt, among other things, with every conceivable issue he would face as governor. On the day he was inaugurated he already had a detailed and ambitious legislative program ready, including a rather mild labor-racketeering bill, a middle-income housing bill based on a wholly original formula, a bill for improving the condition of the beleaguered Manhattan commuters, and much else. To many of the upstate Republicans, the Rockefeller program smelled suspiciously of "creeping socialism." But what really stuck in their gullets was Rockefeller's request for a big tax increase.

Obviously Rockefeller had no desire to increase taxes—he has remarked that he felt like the man who comes in sober at the end of a New Year's Eve party and is handed the bill. But as Norman Hurd has said: "We fed the data into the IBM machines every which way, and it always came out the same: Raise taxes." Rockefeller could no doubt have avoided a tax raise somehow, at least until after the Republican convention in 1960, by cutting back on the services he had promised in his campaign and by further borrowing. Instead, he courageously chose to bite the bullet and to ask not only for a tax increase but for a big one.

Politically, the tax increase hurt him badly. It may have hurt him badly enough to kill his presidential chances, at least for 1960—on that point the reader is again in a better position to judge than the writer. His standing in the public-opinion polls, on which he counts heavily—too heavily—nose-dived. The opinion of the New York taxi drivers was unanimous: "So this rich character gets elected, and right away he's got his hand in my pocket." As Rockefeller has ruefully remarked, raising taxes is bad business for any governor, but it is a lot worse business for a governor named Rockefeller.

A great many Republicans in the legislature felt just as bitterly about Rockefeller's tax increase as the taxi drivers. The result was a Republican revolt, which made it seem likely for a time that Rockefeller's whole legislative program would ingloriously disintegrate. But all observers in Albany agree that the amateur Rockefeller's way of dealing with the revolt was remarkably deft, with a nice feeling for the carrot and the stick.

During the height of the revolt he invited all the key Republican legislators to visit him, in relays, and he treated them to a compelling mixture of charm and sweet reason. "Why, he was a perfect gentleman," one legislator gasped, on emerging from the gubernatorial lair, doubtless recalling Tom Dewey's habit of holding his fellow Republicans' feet to the fire. But Morhouse, Rockefeller's political man Friday, would take over at that point, gently reminding the solons that there was a fire for their feet to be held to. The system worked. Rockefeller got his whole program through without essential change, including the hated tax increase, and even the cynical members of the Albany press corps agree that the first Rockefeller legislative session was a lively and fruitful affair.

Whether it was also a politically suicidal affair remains to be seen. Rockefeller himself did not realize how badly he had been hurt until he was loudly booed, for the first time in his life, at a Manhattan rally. It may be that the hurt is not mortal, and that Rockefeller, like the knight in the Scottish ballad, can lay him doon and bleed awhile, then rise to fight again. There is a built-in reduction of twenty-five per cent in the tax increase, and the revenue provided should give Rockefeller a chance, in this presidential year, to point with pride at a balanced budget and a really striking improvement in the state's services. In any case, Rockefeller's way of dealing with the Republican tax revolt strongly indicates that he has a born politician's instinct for handling other politicians, an instinct which will prove useful if Rockefeller ever becomes President.

Both as regards the executive branch and the Congress, in short, one can confidently predict that Rockefeller would be a "strong President." He would run the show without question in his own branch of the government, and he would use every means at his disposal—not only charm and sweet reason but more practical methods as well—to influence the legislative branch. But to what political end would Rockefeller, as President, use his great power?

At this point, predictions become far less confident. In the 1958 gubernatorial campaign, Tammany boss Carmine De

Sapio said that Rockefeller was "to the left of Franklin Roosevelt." As far as the Republican nomination is concerned, his central weakness, as this is written, is the simple fact that too many regular Republicans agree with De Sapio—to them, Rockefeller does not qualify as a "real Republican."

And it appears to be true that Rockefeller is a good deal to the left of his party. If he had run for the Senate instead of for governor in 1958, New York's balance-of-power Liberal party, to which his wife Tod once belonged, might well have endorsed him. He is personally close to such leaders of the New York Liberals as David Dubinsky and Adolf Berle, and the New York *Post,* which is the bible of the Liberal party and of lower-case liberals as well, endorsed Rockefeller at the last moment in the 1958 campaign.

By any sensible definition, Rockefeller is a lower-case liberal himself. If the word "liberal" means anything these days, it means an internationalist and a big-government man, and Rockefeller is both. He believes, he says, in an "activist" government, by which he means a government which will provide active leadership abroad and which will actively promote the general welfare at home. "Government these days is bigger and more influential than many people realize or like to admit," he told me during the 1958 campaign. "But let's face it—the government is involved in almost every phase of our lives. You've got to recognize that fact first, and accept it, in order to control government, and protect the role of the individual."

Rockefeller believes, in short, that all Americans should have, if not the good things of life he has had, at least the minimum essentials, and that, if need be, it is the government's business to see that they get them. He is a convinced internationalist, as his long losing fight with George Humphrey and company for a more effective foreign-aid program proved, and he gives the national security a higher priority than the budget, as the Rockefeller defense report also proved.

In these and other ways, he fits the current definition of a "liberal."

But there is one way in which he is a genuine conservative. His faith in the capitalist system is unfashionably fervent— he is convinced that it is the best system in the long run, not only for Rockefellers but for everyone. It is this conviction, he has told friends, which has kept him in the Republican party, despite the greener pastures which the Democratic party offers to politically ambitious rich men.

There are other ways, more difficult to define, in which Rockefeller, like most extroverts, is essentially a conservative. Like Nixon, he is in no sense a rebel—he accepts the generally accepted values without seriously questioning them. Conservatives are cautious men, almost by definition, and despite his seeming ebullience and impulsiveness, Rockefeller is a cautious man at heart. It is a special kind of cautiousness, to be sure. "Exciting" and "imaginative" are two of Rockefeller's favorite words, and he likes to do "exciting" and "imaginative" things, like his big investment in IBEC and his decision to run for governor. But before he does one of his exciting and imaginative things, he examines it from every conceivable angle, and he insists on having the best available professional help in the process.

Like his grandfather, in short, Rockefeller is a born looker-before-leaper, a strong believer in "method," who wants to leave "nothing unguessed at, nothing uncounted or unmeasured." One suspects that, in a Rockefeller administration, the headlines would be crowded with "bold, new" proposals and policies, all very "exciting and imaginative," but that these proposals and measures would have been examined minutely and professionally before being permitted to see the light of day.

Otherwise, aside from his faith in capitalism, Rockefeller is not really much interested in ideologies—he is a born pragmatist. Arthur Schlesinger, Jr., the political historian and chief spokesman of the liberal intellectuals, has warned his fellow Democrats that Rockefeller might turn out to be another Theodore Roosevelt, and that he might transform the Republican party into the progressive party, leaving the Democrats with nothing to talk about, as Theodore Roosevelt almost succeeded in doing. If he ever became President, it would certainly be Rockefeller's central political aim to make the Republican party again the normal majority party, as it was before the New Deal. He would use to that end whatever means came to hand, without regard for doctrine or ideology, as Franklin Roosevelt did when he built the strange coalition which is still the majority party, despite the accident of Eisenhower's occupancy of the White House. And he just might succeed.

And although Rockefeller is more frequently compared to Theodore Roosevelt, it is to Franklin Roosevelt, from whom he learned so much, that one returns, in trying to imagine what a Rockefeller presidency might be like. It is hardly a kindness, of course, to compare a man who is suspected, in any case, of not being a "real Republican" to the Republican party's chief devil. And indeed, Rockefeller would be like Franklin Roosevelt only in the sense that Franklin Roosevelt was like his cousin Theodore. As Schlesinger himself has shown, Franklin Roosevelt imitated his distant cousin in many ways, sometimes consciously, sometimes unconsciously. In the same way, Rockefeller's emulation of Franklin Roosevelt is sometimes deliberate and sometimes the unconscious product of similar backgrounds and natures. The end results might be totally different, as the end results of the Franklin Roosevelt presidency were different from those of the presidency of Theodore Roosevelt.

All the same, there are a surprising number of ways in which Rockefeller is like the second Roosevelt. Like Franklin Roosevelt, he is more interested in getting things done than in theories, and in his more cautious way he, too, is an ex-

perimentalist. Like Franklin Roosevelt, Rockefeller is possessed of a kind of nineteenth-century optimism, a conviction
that, if there is a problem, there is somehow, somewhere, a
means of solving it, given an adequate investment of brains
and money and effort. And finally, like Franklin Roosevelt,
beneath a sunny and smiling surface, Nelson Rockefeller is a
most complicated man, at once wily and idealistic, cautious
and bold, tough and tender-hearted, conventional and imaginative. He is a man, like the second Roosevelt, who was
laughed at in his youth as a rich and amiable fool and who
in his maturity is capable of arousing respect, warm admiration and affection, and also fear.

For the rest, no one can possibly predict whether Rockefeller might be a great President, or a good President, or a
disastrous President. It is still too early, after all, to put even
Franklin Roosevelt into one of those three categories with real
assurance. But one can predict that, as President, Rockefeller,
like Roosevelt, would be a political focal point even more
than most Presidents, a large and vital figure dominating the
national and international scene.

Unlike Rockefeller, Nixon is surrounded by no retinue, no
vast entourage. In politics, as in other ways, he is the cat that
walks by himself. Leonard Hall, former chairman of the Republican National Committee, and a shrewd old pro, will
play a big part in the Nixon drive for the White House, but
he is not Nixon's Jim Farley. Nixon is, and always has been,
his own Jim Farley. Nixon has an able press representative,
but he is his own public relations expert. He is even, astonish-
ingly, his own ghost writer. Occasionally an assistant will
draft a Nixon speech, but Nixon himself writes the final draft,
usually in longhand, on his inevitable lawyer's lined, yellow
scratch pads.

Obviously even Nixon, as Vice-President and as presidential candidate, cannot do all his own work. He gets expert help from the three key people in his office staff, Robert Finch, Herbert Klein, and Rosemary Wood. Finch is Nixon's political assistant and alter ego. He is a young lawyer, a former Republican chairman of Los Angeles County—a good-looking man with high cheek bones, a dry sense of humor, and something of Nixon's own watchful self-control. Nixon has said that Finch has the best political brain in his generation, and a conversation with Finch on political matters is almost as enjoyable, to an aficionado of the great game, as a conversation with Nixon. Finch has, in fact, a mind which works almost exactly like Nixon's where politics is concerned —when he expresses a view on some political question, you can be almost morally certain that it is shared by Nixon.[1]

Rosemary Wood, Nixon's confidential secretary, has been Nixon's girl Friday since he was a senator. Like Rockefeller's Louise Boyer, she is much more than a secretary—to use the current gobbledygook of the bureaucracy, she "performs a policy-making function." (During the working day, major politicians seem to need a trustworthy female about. Almost every leading politician has a Rosemary Wood or Louise Boyer. Lyndon Johnson has three or four.) The third key man in the Nixon office is Herbert Klein, a shrewd quiet-voiced newspaperman from southern California, who has performed brilliantly on such occasions as the Russian trip, which was a press representative's nightmare.

All three of these people are very able. If Nixon moves to the White House, all three are likely to move with him. In that case they will be powerful people, but their power will not be independent—it will be an extension of Nixon's power.

[1] *This phenomenon of the political alter ego is not unusual; Senator Johnson has an alter ego in Bobby Baker, secretary of the Senate Majority Leader, and Senator Kennedy has another in his administrative assistant, Ted Thorenson.*

There is a boss-employee relationship between Nixon and his office triumvirate which is subtly different from the more personal relationship between Rockefeller and his Inner Circle.

Outside his office, those closest to Nixon are probably Attorney General William Rogers, James Bassett, Ted Rogers, a television executive, and Jack Drown, an old poker-playing friend. Of the four the first three were on the Nixon train when the fund crisis broke, and they are members of the Nixon-created Order of the Hound's Tooth. There is a special relationship between Nixon and those who were with him in the great crisis of his life, rather like the relationship between veterans of the same battle.

In the Eisenhower cabinet the men closest to Nixon, other than his friend Rogers, are Secretary of Labor Mitchell and Secretary of State Herter. Nixon and Mitchell have often been on the same side of the fence in policy debates within the Administration—significantly, since Mitchell is markedly the most liberal Eisenhower administration cabinet member. Mitchell is a Catholic and an easterner, and a Nixon-Mitchell ticket is a distinct possibility, especially if Senator Kennedy is not the Democratic presidential candidate. (The logic here is that the Catholics will vote for Kennedy anyway if he is the Democratic standard-bearer, but if he is turned down, Mitchell will attract Catholic votes to the Republican ticket.) Nixon first knew Herter when he served on the Herter committee, and despite the Stassen farce, they have been friendly ever since.

If Nixon becomes President, Herter and possibly Secretary of the Interior Fred Seaton might be asked to stay on. Mitchell and Rogers would be almost certain of some sort of important post. Perhaps Attorney General Summerfield would also get a good job, for Nixon has not forgotten Summerfield's stubborn championship of his cause during the fund crisis. Otherwise there would probably be no Eisenhower holdovers.

Among others around Nixon, Murray Chotiner is in a special category. Nixon makes no bones about his admiration for Chotiner's political judgment, and if Chotiner were vindicated by being elected to Congress he would probably have far more access to the White House in a Nixon administration than most freshman congressmen. Also in a special category is Philip Watts, Nixon's perambulating conscience and occasional golfing companion. That about completes the list.

With the exception of Jack Drown (who will replace the perennial George Allen as official presidential crony if Nixon is elected) and the possible exception of Watts, Nixon's friendships are what is known on Madison Avenue as "business friendships." They are associations connected with Nixon's political career. This is true even of Rogers. Like Finch, Rogers shares Nixon's passion for politics, and he, too, thinks politically much as Nixon thinks. Politics made Rogers and Nixon friends, and keeps them friends.

But although they are friends, and Nixon listens to his advice, Rogers does not have a decisive influence on Nixon. Nixon is so much his own man that no one, no one at all, has a really decisive influence on him. In a Nixon administration there would be no Colonel House, no Harry Hopkins, no Sherman Adams. As President, Nixon would also demand, and get, "positive loyalty" in the executive branch, but loyalty of a far less personal sort than Rockefeller would demand. Unlike Rockefeller, Nixon does not much care whether his subordinates like him, so long as they do what he wants them to do, and do it well.

Nixon is, in short, more interested in results than affection, which also suggests how a President Nixon would handle his relations with Capitol Hill. Nixon has never been a "Senate man" or a member of what journalist William White has dubbed "The Inner Club." No cozy groups congregate in the Vice-President's office late in the afternoon to "strike a blow for liberty," as they did when Alben Barkley or Jack Garner held the office.

Nixon is no parliamentarian—he has never really learned the great body of rulings and precedents which a true Senate man must master. In this respect, Majority Leader Lyndon Johnson can make Nixon, as presiding officer, look like a fool —on one embarrassing occasion, involving a Nixon ruling on Senate Rule 22, Johnson did just that. All the same, Nixon understands Congress. He understands how the system works, why representatives and senators vote as they do—after all, he has been both himself. Indeed, since his political career started in 1946, Nixon has had continuous experience in what makes Congress tick—or fail to tick—and that is an asset which Rockefeller entirely lacks.

On the other hand, Nixon lacks the easy, arm-on-the-shoulder camaraderie of Rockefeller—and charm, as Franklin Roosevelt proved, can be a potent weapon in the ancient running battle between the executive and legislative branches. In any case, Nixon, like Rockefeller, would be a "strong President," which means that he would fight, like a tigress defending her cubs, against congressional encroachment on the presidential prerogatives, while using every means at his disposal to dominate the Congress.

Would Nixon be a "liberal" or a "conservative" President? Up to this point we have been on fairly solid ground, but here the ground is soft and boggy. For one thing, it is becoming increasingly difficult to define just what the two words mean in terms of actual legislation. For another, Nixon's record is not consistent. In his first term in the House he voted like a down-the-line doctrinaire right-wing Republican. Thereafter he began a gentle movement toward the center, which has continued, with some zigs and zags, ever since. In the interview reproduced in the appendix, when I remarked that it seemed to me he was a "conservative, in terms of respect for the status quo," Nixon betrayed some irritation

—naturally enough, no doubt, since it is always irritating to be told what you think by somebody else—and listed such areas as medical care, aid to education, and civil rights, in which he considered his views liberal.

Yet I still believe that Nixon is an instinctive conservative, just as he was the kind of boy who instinctively accepted the conventional standards of the world as he found it. But he lacks the passionate, doctrinaire conservatism of a man like George Humphrey, whose thinking continued to dominate the Eisenhower administration even after he ceased to be Secretary of the Treasury. There is nothing sacred to Nixon about a balanced budget, as he demonstrated when he unsuccessfully advocated a tax cut during the 1958 recession.

In the area of foreign and defense policy, Nixon's record has been more consistent, and is easier to read, than in any other area. Ever since the Herter committee days, as noted earlier, he has been a strong advocate of foreign aid, with no visible political profit to himself. He is an internationalist, an activist, an interventionist—call it what you will—in foreign policy. As he says, "I would take chances for peace." His record on defense is also consistent—up to a point. He has voted for a strong defense, and within the Administration, especially in the era immediately after the Sputniks, he argued for an increased defense effort. But in 1959, as we have seen, he reversed himself and strongly supported the Administration against criticism of its inadequate defense program.

His motives were certainly at least in part political—if he had not supported the President on that issue, the President might have intervened against his nomination. And this suggests another prediction which can be made with some assurance about Nixon as President. He would be a thoroughly political President. In Robert Donovan's revealing book about the Eisenhower administration, *Eisenhower: The Inside Story,* Nixon always plays the same role. When an issue is up for discussion, Nixon shrewdly sums up the probable

political impact of alternative courses of action—he very
rarely comments on the inherent merits of the issue in question. As President, Nixon would look beyond politics, but
politics would still be very much on his mind.

Politics was rarely absent from the mind of Franklin Roosevelt, and Harry Truman was not precisely non-partisan. A
good case can be made for the view that one of Dwight Eisenhower's gravest weaknesses as President has been his lack
of practical political experience. A thoroughly political President, in short, is by no means necessarily a bad President.
Nor does it seem to me that the inconsistency of Nixon's
stands on certain issues is as damning as his critics maintain.
A doctrinaire consistency like Senator Taft's can, indeed, be
a very dangerous quality in a President. It is fortunate that
Lincoln's later policies were not consistent with his pre-Civil
War views on slavery, and that Franklin Roosevelt was not
consistently faithful to his 1932 campaign pledges.

For the rest, one can only guess. In one way, at least, it
seems a fair guess that Nixon would be a less conservative
President than Rockefeller—for he is at heart a less cautious
man. "I'm always willing to take a chance," he says. "I think
that has been the mark of my political career." Nixon, to be
sure, like Rockefeller, always weighs the risks carefully in advance. But he relies far more on his own intuition than on
"studies" or expert analyses. The next four years are certain
to be a time of continuing crisis, whoever may be President.
One can imagine Nixon, far more easily than Rockefeller, deliberately deciding "to take a chance" at a time of great international crisis in order to turn the crisis to the West's
advantage, as he turned the fund crisis, for example, to his
own advantage.

It is true that there are still intelligent people, who are not
partisan or doctrinaire Democrats and who have in their
minds a small pea of doubt about Nixon, who fear that, in
his fierce ambition and his total absorption in politics, he

might pervert the enormous powers of the presidency to his own political ends. And it is obviously impossible to predict what effect the office of the presidency would have on Nixon, or what effect Nixon would have on that office.

But Nixon has grown already, since the days when he saw winning elections by whatever means as the chief function of a politician, and surely the chances are that if he became President he would grow further in office, as almost all Presidents have grown. And certain of the qualities which Nixon has displayed in his political career—the boldness and decisiveness, the instinct for "moving quickly to shape events," the sure feel for the realities of power, the strong intelligence, the cool toughness and simple guts in time of crisis—would also be markedly useful in a President.

And so the portraits of these two men are as complete as I know how to make them. I realize that they are incomplete, that there are areas which are dim and fuzzy, or almost blank, because I have not explored them, or because I have not understood. I realize also that, although I have tried to write fairly about Rockefeller and Nixon, without special pleading or prejudice, I have not entirely succeeded. Perhaps it is not possible to be entirely fair about living politicians—no one who is not a political eunuch is without political prejudice. Some readers will certainly feel strongly that I have been too kind to one or the other or both, and others will feel just as strongly that I have not been kind enough. As I noted at the beginning, what looks to me like a wen or pimple may look to someone else like a beauty mark, and vice versa.

In any case, it is not up to the writer to decide whether Rockefeller or Nixon is better suited to the presidency, or whether the Democrats have a candidate who is better suited to that office than either of them. The curious, cumbersome, unique American political process will make those choices, and the chances are really very good that the choices will be well and truly made. For odd as it seems to foreigners, our political process works, on balance, remarkably well. It not only works well in making the ultimate choice for the presidential office but also in producing unusual and interesting men from among whom to choose. And surely those adjectives fit Richard Milhous Nixon and Nelson Aldrich Rockefeller.

Appendix

A Talk with Nixon

Author's note:

The following talk with Nixon seems to me to give a
rather vivid impression of Nixon talking, off the cuff, to an
audience of one. The talk was not tape-recorded (tape-
recording seems to me to take all the art out of interviewing)
and it is therefore not absolutely verbatim. But I wrote it all
down as soon as I had left Nixon, and although my memory
is notoriously bad in other ways, it is briefly phonographic,
and the talk is entirely accurate in substance. Excerpts have
appeared in the Saturday Evening Post, but the talk seems
to me to have a cumulative impact and to be worth reproducing in full.

There is no comparable talk with Rockefeller available. I
have had a number of interviews with him, but he insisted
that he should not be directly quoted.

S.A.

Large stone house. Pleasant porch overlooking Glover Park. Coffee. A little chitchat about how Ike likes a heaping spoonful of sugar in his coffee, and how Route 240 is going through the Park but won't be visible. But Nixon is no small talker, so down to business.

ALSOP: The thing that's impressed me most in my reporting on you is your extraordinary energy, ambition, drive, call it what you will. One of your law-school classmates remembers you as the hardest working man he's ever met. Now, this is a rather introspective question and may be impossible to answer. But how did you get that way? Your Quaker background, your family, your economic circumstances as a boy, or what?

NIXON: Well, I suppose it was a mixture of all the factors you mention. There was always a tradition of hard work in my family, especially my mother's side, the Quaker side. My grandmother on my mother's side was an extraordinary woman. She died at ninety-two—she came all the way across the country in a 1930 Chevrolet at the age of eighty-eight to see me graduate from Duke Law School. She used to write poetry a lot—she'd make up her own poems for birthday cards and Christmas cards and so on. In a sort of gentle Quaker way she was always trying to inspire us all to amount to something.

Then there was my father. He had a tough time as a boy, very tough. He had to leave school early—fifth or sixth grade—and go to work. He worked on a farm for seven years, and he liked to tell us about it, hard work for almost nothing. But he saved everything he had—he had to, to become independent. He was a very competitive man. He always instilled this competitive feeling in all of us—I guess I acquired my competitive instinct from him. He was a fighter. He loved to argue with anybody about anything. I remember my first debate, in fifth grade at school. The subject was "Resolved, that it is better to own your own home than to rent." I was on the renting side. Father sat down and did a lot of figuring and proved that it was more economical to rent than to own—he very much wanted me to win.

My mother had a lot to do with my doing well at school, too. She is a very capable woman. She never finished college, but she had German and Latin and she still remembers a lot of it. It was because of her that I got straight As in four years of high-school Latin.

Then there was the illness in my family. My older brother died of tuberculosis and the illness was very expensive. We all worked like hell—we had to. There was a drive to succeed, to survive almost. My mother and father instilled in us the desire to get going, to be good not just at one single thing but at everything. Take science, I hated science, not the theoretical end but the mathematical side—I liked the experiments. But I worked hard at it and did better than most. We had a disciplined family—we always had to clean up our plates at a meal. My father was a real disciplinarian.

ALSOP: I've heard him described as "cantankerous."

NIXON: Yes, that's right. My mother is the complete opposite. My mother is the gentlest, most considerate woman—I suppose everybody thinks that about his mother, but it's true. She never turned a tramp away from the door. That was one of the things she and my dad used to argue about. My father thought they ought to be made to work before helping them out. But Mother ran the house like a charitable operation. We had to have somebody working for us, because we were all working at the store. Looking back, I think we had more people who did less, working for us, than any other house.

ALSOP: Did the fact that you grew up during the Depression have anything to do with this drive of yours?

NIXON: I suppose in some ways. It's been said our family was poor, and maybe it was, but we never thought of ourselves as poor. We always had enough to eat, and we never had to depend on anyone else. Sure, we had to be careful. I was dressed in hand-me-downs mostly in grammar school. Once in a while we'd go to a movie, but that was a luxury. We never had any vacations—well, once in a long while we'd have a week at the beach, maybe. But I never went hunting or fishing or anything like that—there wasn't time. We never ate out—never. We certainly had to learn the value of money. But we had a pretty good time, with it all.

Then there was the atmosphere of the times, of course. One of my jobs at the store was to add up the bills on an adding machine. We had to carry a lot of people on credit—sometimes for years—and I saw at firsthand the problem of people who couldn't pay their bills, who were out of a job.

But it was a sort of tradition in our family that whatever you did you had to do as well as you could. I was a lousy football player, but I remember Chief Newman, our football coach, saying "there's one thing about Nixon, he plays every scrimmage as though the championship were at stake." That's the competitive characteristic—I suppose it goes back to my dad.

ALSOP: Another thing about you is your instinct for politics. Mrs. Nixon once wrote in the *Post* that "Dick can think about politics and work at it every hour of the day"—something like that. You yourself once described yourself as "a political animal." How did you get that way?

NIXON: Well, again, I suppose my dad had something to do with it. He had no business succeeding in business. He'd argue with anybody at the drop of a hat about politics. He used to argue with my mother because she was strong for Woodrow Wilson. She voted for Wilson in 1916, because he was for peace. My father used to point out that we got into the war anyway, but that didn't change Mother.

In 1924 my father was very strong for La Follette. Then in 1928 he was very much for Hoover. You remember Hoover then was the liberal candidate. My family was very strong for Hoover in 1928 and in 1932.

ALSOP: Did the fact that Hoover was a Quaker have any-thing to do with it?

NIXON: Yes, of course. My father was a converted Quaker, became a Quaker after he married Mother. He taught Sun-day school. We used to go to church four times a day on Sunday—Sunday school, then church, then Christian Educa-tion, then church in the evening. Also prohibition was an issue in 1928 and 1932, and that had an influence. My grand-mother was a charter member of the WCTU. Al Smith's reli-gion never had anything to do with it though. I wasn't even aware of his religion—my mother would never have permitted it. There's the Quaker tradition of tolerance. Racial tolerance, too. We used to have Negroes and Mexicans working for us sometimes, and we always ate at the same table—never thought of anything else. A Quaker custom.

ALSOP: I'd heard your father voted for F.D.R. in 1932.

NIXON: No, not in 1932, in 1936. He was strong for Roosevelt in 1936, I remember.

ALSOP: Now here's something of a crystal-ball question. You're a politician, of course, a professional politician—your critics say you're too much of a politician. Have you ever thought about the function of a politician in our kind of society?

NIXON: The function of a politician is to make a free society work. When I've been abroad, I've been impressed often how men with good intentions and high ideals without political experience often fail when they try their hand at the practical business of government—take Indonesia, for example, Burma.

When I first ran in 1946 I was a bit naïve about public service, a kind of dragon slayer, I suppose.

ALSOP: "Mr. Smith Goes to Washington" sort of thing?

NIXON: Yes, yes—I remember that movie well. Jerry Voorhis was supposed to be Mr. Smith, you know. Then when I got to Washington I was soon disillusioned. You know, you come to Washington, you have great ideas, and there you are in the

committees and on the floor of the House, and you have an
inability to implement your ideas. You see men who are—
well, I don't want to sound pious but—less well motivated,
say, and who know how to play the game, and they accomplish what they want. Then there are the Don Quixotes, who
never accomplish anything, the idealistic men—like Jerry
Voorhis. One of my campaign points in that first campaign
was that Jerry Voorhis had introduced 126 bills and he had
only one piece of legislation with his name on it. Of course,
when I got to Washington I realized soon it wasn't easy to
get through legislation with your name on it.

Anyway, I suppose there was scarcely ever a man with
higher ideals than Jerry Voorhis, or better motivated than
Jerry Voorhis. But he couldn't get anything through. You've
got to learn how to play the game, if you're going to implement your ideas, and you've got to fight it out.

You've got to be a politician before you can become a
statesman—a lot of people have said that before me. You get
here, and you've got to learn how to operate—the boring and
frustrating committee system, and so on. You find often
you've got to take a half a loaf when you want the whole
loaf. There's a quotation that expresses what I mean exactly.
(Puts hand to head to try to recall it) It's in my office, I'll
have them send it to you. Some German—was it Bismarck?
No, I don't think so. It goes something like this: "The way to
punish any country or principality is to allow it to be governed by philosophers."

The best example of a combination of idealist and practical
politician is Theodore Roosevelt. When he wanted to get
something done, he would compromise all over the place.
Read the autobiography of Bob La Follette. He throws off on
T.R., says he's not a true liberal because he compromised too
much. But who accomplished more, Roosevelt or La Follette?
Or Bowers of India—he came from Indiana, so he was more
practical than La Follette, but he throws off on Theodore

Roosevelt, too. T.R. was always saying that men of good back-ground—men of wealth, he called it—should not sit around in their clubs talking about how terrible things are, but should get into the hurly-burly.

Working for the OPA before the war was a great experi-ence for me. You know the man I worked for was Dave Lloyd. I suppose he thinks I'm terrible now. But I certainly worked hard, on tire rationing, for example, trying to prevent people from getting away with murder.

You know the hardest thing for me in politics is to go and ask for a job, I just can't do it. Political jobs come to me be-cause I happen to be there. Back in Whittier I became a mem-ber of the board of the college after Duke Law School—it was unheard of, having anyone so young as a member of the board, but they decided they needed young blood and I was there. Then in 1940 the assemblyman from our district was retiring, this was just before Pearl Harbor. I had been presi-dent of the 20-30 Club and active in Kiwanis, and I'd made some speeches for Willkie—very bad speeches—and they talked about running me for the Assembly. Now I don't mean I'm a shrinking violet in politics. I'm always ready—public service has always appealed to me more than making money. But I do have this aversion to going up to a stranger, or some-one I don't know well, and asking for political support or a contribution.

I remember in 1952 when Bob Taft came to my office and said he would like my support for the nomination. I explained why I was for Eisenhower, and Taft, who was a big man, didn't resent it. But for me that would have been terribly dif-ficult—I could never go to a senator, to his office, and ask for his support. With me, the way I work is different. It's a matter of being in the right place at the right time.

That's how I was elected president of the student body at Duke, for example—Leon Price was in the class ahead of me, and he was looking for a candidate to run from the Iredell

Club, one of the two clubs, and he asked me if I'd like to run for the president of the Bar Association.

Now I don't mean I'm above seeking office, or the maneuvers and machinations involved. And I'm always willing to take a chance. I think that has been the mark of my political career. In 1950, for example, all my friends, almost all, urged me not to run for the Senate, since I had a safe seat in the House. It looked as though Sheridan Downey would run again, and he looked almost impossible to beat. If I'd stayed in the House, maybe I'd have been Speaker eventually. But I decided to take the chance. Then Downey withdrew, and Helen Gahagan Douglas was easier to beat. But when I went for it, I thought it would be Downey.

Maybe it's that old poker-playing instinct.

ALSOP: You mean, to know when to go for broke?

NIXON: Yes, that's it.

ALSOP: Naturally I've done a lot of reporting about the famous fund dispute. One thing that's impressed me is that nobody sensed that the fund might be a political booby trap. That wasn't surprising in the case of the businessmen who contributed. But Chotiner, Jim Bassett, they knew about the fund, and they certainly aren't politically naïve. Or yourself, for that matter.

NIXON: Yes. Most successful politicians had state committees and special funds to take care of mailings and broadcasts and so on.

ALSOP: So your first reaction when the fund story broke was simple unconcern?

NIXON: Yes, the best proof of that was when Pete Edson first asked about the fund, and I gave him the telephone number of Dana Smith, the treasurer, and told him he could get all the details from Smith.

ALSOP: Then it seems to me you had two further reactions. Your second reaction was to say you'd been smeared, after you saw signs like one Bill Rogers told me about—PAT,

WHAT ARE YOU GOING TO DO WITH THE BRIBE MONEY?

NIXON: Yes, there were worse ones than that.

ALSOP: And then you realized that it wouldn't be enough to say you'd been smeared, and you'd have to fight back.

NIXON: Yes, I guess the worst thing was when the New York *Herald Tribune* called on me to resign. The Washington *Post* didn't bother me so much—it had been critical of me always, for example, the Alger Hiss case. But the *Tribune* was different—Bert Andrews' paper, my friend. Then there were telegrams—from Harold Stassen, for example—asking me to withdraw. Have you seen Stassen's telegrams? You ought to.

ALSOP: And Tom Dewey called you—"I hate to say this, Dick," and so on.

NIXON: Yes, it's been said I'd never forgive the people who wanted me to get off, but that's not true. In perspective, you can see why they did it. The big issue was the mess in Washington, and I seemed to be blunting that issue.

I had a debate with myself those first days. I really think it was not basically personal. I put great weight on the possibility that if I did not withdraw it might result in the defeat of Eisenhower. I talked a lot with Pat, and Hillings, and Chotiner.

ALSOP: Pat wanted you to get out, didn't she? I've heard that from several people.

NIXON: No, maybe later, but not then. I was discouraged and disgusted, and I told her that my withdrawing might assure Eisenhower's election. She said two things: "Look, if you get off, you will carry the scar for the rest of your life. It will look as though you had been forced off." That was her first point, and her second was: "If you get off, Ike will lose."

Hillings took a different line. He's a Catholic and strong anti-Communist, of course, and he kept saying that if I got off the ticket all my enemies who had been trying to get me

—he was talking about the far left, of course—all these people would gloat.

It was a great strain. I am seldom emotional in public, it does not pay, you should never allow your temper to break, but of course it was an emotional strain privately. I did what I always do. I considered all the worst alternatives, as cold-bloodedly as I could, and I made an analytical decision—that if I withdrew, Ike would probably lose. So I decided to make the effort to stay on, if possible with honor.

ALSOP: I've talked to a lot of people about your telephone conversation with Eisenhower, on the Sunday before the broadcast. I think I have a pretty accurate picture of it, and I'm impressed by the fact that your attitude was certainly not meek or defensive. As I get it, you told the General that you would get off if he, and the Republican National Committee, thought you ought to, but that he and the country ought to hear your side of the case first. You warned him against listening to some of the people around him who didn't know anything about it. You said the decision had to be made as quickly as possible, otherwise it would harm the whole ticket. And you concluded by saying, in effect, "In politics, General, the time comes when you've got to pee or get off the pot."

NIXON: Well, that last sentence may be part of the mythology. After all, there were only two people who heard the conversation, me and the General.

ALSOP: I understood there were three or four people in the room with you.

NIXON: Maybe, I don't remember. Anyway, you have it about right. I told the General, as we called him then, that, if you want, I'll get off the ticket. He said: "This is not my decision, it is yours." And I said I'd be glad to take the responsibility either way. I said I thought I should make my side of the case publicly, and that if after all it was decided I shouldn't stay on the ticket, I'd take the responsibility for withdrawing. Then I did say, though I don't remember saying exactly what you said, that the worst thing you could do was to delay, that in this sort of situation you had to kill the story as quickly as possible.

In the whole fund matter Chotiner was the strongest of all —like a rock. It was a tragedy that he had to get involved in the kind of law business that does not mix with politics.

ALSOP: I had a long talk with him in California. He's an interesting man. A straight political technician. He has no interest at all in the issues themselves.

NIXON: No, but he knows which issues are good and bad. And he said again and again: "If you get off, Eisenhower will lose."

ALSOP: I wanted to talk to you about another aspect of the fund row that seemed to me particularly interesting. I got this from both ends. According to this version, you were emotionally drained after the broadcast, and you got a version of Eisenhower's telegram to you telling you to come to Wheeling as a help to him in the "formulation of his decision," and so on. The telegram was obviously equivocal and suggested he still had not made up his mind to keep you on the ticket. According to what I heard, you then sat down and wrote out a telegram resigning, which Chotiner intercepted and tore up.

NIXON: Well, something like that might have been discussed. It's true we were pretty emotional after the broadcast, and we got only a part of the General's telegram over the radio, not the congratulatory part, and we were pretty distressed. But I don't think any telegram resigning was ever sent out—I never had any serious intention of withdrawing. I knew by then the broadcast was a success—Darryl Zanuck had wired me that it was wonderful, for example, and I had a lot of confidence in his judgment. My concern throughout was motivated by a cold-blooded political judgment of what was best for the ticket, and that was why it was a pretty emotional talk.

ALSOP: You went on to Missoula, didn't you, instead of flying right away to Wheeling.

NIXON: Yes, Chotiner insisted on that. He was even against my going to Los Angeles to make the speech. He insisted we must not make it appear that we were thrown off stride by this maneuver by the enemy—we must take it in our stride.

ALSOP: Some of your friends think that the crisis had a major effect on you—like an infantryman who's been through a bad battle—nothing in your political life could be worse.

NIXON: Well, it was certainly an emotional load. Just before the broadcast I had my worst moment—I turned to Pat and said: "You know, I don't think I can go through with it —I don't think I can make the speech."

I developed most of my ideas riding down on the plane from Portland. I remember I began to get ideas, and I reached ahead and picked out those postcards they have on planes and wrote down my ideas on them, to be sorted out later. Like the quotation from Lincoln.

ALSOP: Or the dog Checkers?

NIXON: Yes.

ALSOP: Did you have Fala in mind?

NIXON: Of course I did. I got a kind of malicious pleasure out of it. I'll needle them on this one, I said to myself.

ALSOP: I was amused looking back through old Whittier yearbooks. It seemed to me I found the ancestor of that "respectable Republican cloth coat"—you remember the pictures of the Franklins and the Orthogonians?

NIXON: Sure, sure, the open collars. They were the haves, and we were the have nots, see? I was just a freshman then.

ALSOP: It must have been quite a trick starting a new college club as a mere freshman.

NIXON: I don't want to take all the credit. The original idea was Dean Trigg's a year ahead of me. I wrote the club song and the constitution and so on. But about the speech, I will say no speech could have been more difficult. After that I could never develop stage fright again. And I suppose the whole experience was aging. I was only thirty-nine then.

The more you stay in this kind of job, the more you realize that a public figure, a major public figure, is a lonely man— the President very much more so, of course. But even in my job you can't enjoy the luxury of intimate personal friendships. You can't confide absolutely in anyone. You can't talk too much about your personal plans, your personal feelings. I believe in keeping my own counsel. It's something like wearing clothing—if you let down your hair, you feel too naked.

I remember when I'd just started law practice, I had a divorce case to handle, and this good-looking girl, beautiful, really, began talking to me about her intimate marriage problems.

ALSOP: And you were embarrassed?

NIXON: Embarrassed? I turned fifteen colors of the rainbow. I suppose I came from a family too unmodern, really. Any kind of personal confession is embarrassing to me generally. I can discuss the issues, general subjects. I have fun playing poker, being with friends. But any letting down my hair, I find that embarrassing.

ALSOP: I was amused, because several of your law-school contemporaries wrote me that they thought you were "shy" —odd word for a successful professional politician.

NIXON: Yes, that's still true in a way. Take raising money. I can make a speech to thousands, to ten million on television, but I can no more go up to a single individual and ask for a ten-dollar political contribution than I can fly. I can sell in the mass. But asking some individual to vote my way, for example, I'm no good at that. I suppose it is shyness, in a way.

ALSOP: Now for the case against Nixon—I couldn't write honestly without considering the case against Nixon. Take the 1946 campaign first. The case against you in 1946 boils down to the charge that you attempted to identify Jerry Voorhis as the "PAC candidate," when in fact he wasn't endorsed by the California PAC, which was Communist controlled, because he was anti-Communist.

NIXON: The NC-PAC did endorse him. The NC-PAC and the CIO-PAC were almost the same thing. They shared office space here, and most of the same officers. Communism was not an issue in 1946, despite what people have said later. I remember, for example, I never raised the issue that Voorhis had voted against the Un-American Activities Committee—at that time I didn't think too much of the committee myself.

ALSOP: But in Helen Douglas's campaign, the charge against you, in her words, is that you tried to make people believe she was a "Communist or communistic." There was the famous pink sheet, for example.

NIXON: You've got to put that campaign in the context of the time—1950 and the Korean War. I never said or implied that Helen Douglas was a Communist. I specifically said she was not. I did charge her with a lack of understanding of the basic issue of communism. I think the charge was accurate. She belonged to several Communist-front organizations—we had documentary proof. As for the pink sheet, the key vote there was her vote against Greek-Turkish aid. We really had her on the hook when Truman's Attorney General, McGrath, came out and praised her for supporting the Truman doctrine for stopping communism. We never let her off that hook, pointing out that I had voted for Greek-Turkish aid and she against it.

Sure it was a rough campaign. It was rough two ways. They called me a tool of the vested interests, a Fascist. I was picketed by Communists—not all Communists, of course, Wallace supporters and such, they gave me a rough time. I gave it back. I believe in giving as good as you get. Take her vote against the Un-American Activities Committee. That didn't prove she was a Communist or pro-Communist. But it did prove something else. That however well intentioned, she didn't understand the big issue.

ALSOP: Take your famous rhetorical question about Dulles and Acheson—"Isn't it wonderful finally to have a Secretary of State who isn't taken in by the Communists?" That may have been legitimate as a debater's point, but I don't think it was legitimate coming from someone in your position.

NIXON: Don't forget that was said in the context of a debate, when Stevenson and Acheson were going after Dulles and Eisenhower. I was defending them in the context of their foreign policies. I believe in hitting back.

ALSOP: Yes, but I believe that the case against you boils down to the fact that your experience as a college debater has carried over into your career as a politician. It is a college debater's function to score debating points, often specious ones, against the opposition. But a politician's function, especially a Vice-President's, is a lot more than that.

NIXON: (thoughtfully) Yes, that may be a legitimate criticism. When somebody launches an attack, your instinct is to strike back. I think I have developed a more subtle response now, to finesse an attack. I counsel younger politicians to ignore attacks, take a positive line.

Even so, I don't believe in letting the opposition select the battleground, either domestically or internationally.

Take Khrushchev and the leaders of international communism. How did they qualify? By clawing their way up through the Communist jungle, fighting every inch of the way. We've got to realize that, besides being entirely ruthless, these men are very, very able. I don't believe in adopting their methods. But I don't believe in adopting a strictly defensive attitude, either, letting them select the battlefield every time. We've got to respond in our own way. If you're always on the defensive, you always lose in the end.

ALSOP: Tell me, how did you feel in Peru and Venezuela, when you realized you were in real physical danger? Were you scared?

NIXON: How did I feel? Well, that's hard to describe. Generally speaking, my reaction—to stress, a challenge, some great difficulty—is sort of chemically delayed. While it is going on, I feel cold, matter of fact, analytical. At Lima, for example, when I saw the mob before the university, I made the decision to get out of the car and walk up to the mob on foot. I tried to analyze each face, to separate the Communists from the neutrals or the friendly ones. And I kept asking, "Where is your leader?" It was deliberately calculated to put the Communists on the spot. Then when I saw the soft answer would not work, that they wouldn't let me speak, I allowed myself the luxury of showing my temper and calling them cowards. It was deliberate, letting my temper show— not that I didn't really feel it; it was a terrible thing these Communists were doing, using these poor, often ignorant people in that way. Then after a crisis like that is over, I feel this tremendous letdown, a fatigue, as though I'd been in a battle.

ALSOP: Here's a tough one to answer—how do you see yourself in the political spectrum, between left and right? My own view is that you're an instinctive conservative, in terms of respect for the status quo, but at the same time a flexible and highly practical conservative.

NIXON: You're talking about domestic affairs only, or international affairs? Because I'm not necessarily a respecter of the status quo in foreign affairs. I am a chance-taker in foreign affairs. I would take chances for peace—the Quakers have a passion for peace, you know. I think my record on foreign affairs is directed to an understanding of the meaning of international communism—I see the Communist danger at home as part of a foreign-policy threat primarily.

On domestic matters I'm, of course, partly influenced by my early upbringing. I have a strong emotional feeling for the problems of what I'd call ordinary people; I've known unemployed people, for example, and I know what their problems are. I've always taken an advanced position on medical care; we had that terrible sickness in my family, and I know the medical problems ordinary families face. Then again, because of my own experience, I feel very strongly about educational opportunities for people in the lower brackets. I would say I was not especially conservative as regards civil rights; again, that is a matter of family feelings, we have a strong family tradition against discrimination. But in some other ways I suppose I am conservative, yes.

ALSOP: Like Senator Kennedy and other Democrats, I think you would be a formidable candidate for the presidency, not only because you're a formidable campaigner but because you've proved your intelligence and ability in the vice-presidency. But I think you have two weaknesses as a presidential candidate. This is only my opinion, of course, but perhaps you'd like to comment on it. One weakness is that too many people consider you an extremist, a radical—they identify you with McCarthy and the extreme right. The other is more intangible. It is that the public image of you lacks warmth, and depth, and humanness. To most people you're too much a cardboard figure.

NIXON: I'm fatalistic about politics. You can't go out and push for the presidency. It's a matter of the right man in the right place at the right time. You can't run for the presidency —look at Bob Taft, or Harold Stassen. . . .

ALSOP: Or Kefauver?

NIXON: Yes, the presidency seeks the man, not the other way around. Those two points you raised will be answered by what happens. On the first point, about my being an extremist, I think that has been partly answered already. I know the Democrats will try to picture me as an extremist. But you can't go on hashing up the distant past indefinitely.

On the second point, well, there are some things you can't do anything about. You've got to be what you are, you can't pretend to be something different. Anyway, what happens is in the lap of the Fates.

It depends what the times call for. If the time comes when the Republican party and the voters are looking for an outwardly warm, gregarious, easygoing type——

ALSOP: A backslapper——

NIXON: Yes—then they will not want the sort of man I am. But these are serious times, and they may not call for that kind of personality. All our Presidents haven't been personality boys, after all.

ALSOP: Woodrow Wilson?

NIXON: Yes, but he had a great reputation as an intellectual.

ALSOP: Or Franklin Roosevelt—he wasn't really a warm personality, essentially a cold man. . . .

NIXON: Was he? I never met him. But he projected warmth. . . . You know, I suppose I'm about the only major public figure who's never had a public relations expert. I write all my own speeches. I make up my own mind what to say. On my trips abroad, everything successful I did was over the objections of the State Department.

A lot of people have told me, what you need is a public relations expert. They tell me I ought to look at kinescopes of my television appearances to improve my speeches. You know, I've never heard a speech I've made played back, never seen myself on television. The reason is that I don't want to seem artificial. I think a television speaker ought to be natural, uninhibited, as though he were having a conversation with the audience. Naturally, sometimes you talk louder than in a conversation, more earnestly, with more emphasis. But you've got to be natural.

I do meet a great number of people, and part of the image of me as cold or withdrawn is false, I think, partly as a result of the press. But it is true that I'm fundamentally relatively shy. It doesn't come natural to me to be a buddy-buddy boy. When I meet a lot of people, I tend to seek out the shy ones. Anyway, I'm not going to have a lot of high-powered public relations people working on me to humanize me, with pictures of me doing silly things and so on.

It will depend on the times. If the times require a tough-minded, objective man—objective about the facts here and abroad—incisive, hard-working, a man who can handle himself on the international scene—now, I'm not describing myself necessarily—but if that is the public temper then, that is the kind of man the public will get.

ALSOP: Well, I've taken up a lot of your time already. Thanks very much—it's been really interesting.

NIXON: (returning to former theme) You know, I try to be candid with newspapermen, but I can't really let my hair down with anyone.

ALSOP: Not even with old friends, like the Jack Drowns, say?

NIXON: No, not really with anyone, not even with my family. But I have fun with friends like the Jack Drowns. That is one thing people are wrong about—I can have as good a time as anybody.

A little chitchat about the house at the front door—how it used to belong to Homer Cummings—and good-bys.

Rockefeller: Dartmouth

Author's note:

What follows is a selection of excerpts from letters I received from classmates of Nelson Rockefeller at Dartmouth and from classmates of Richard Nixon at Whittier High School, Whittier College, and Duke University Law School.

It seems to me that these excerpts are worth preserving. Indeed, to anyone interested in these two remarkable men, the letters are oddly revealing—one catches a sudden vivid glimpse of the boys they used to be, as in an old photograph album. The Nixon letters seem to me more interesting than the Rockefeller letters—Rockefeller was so universally liked that the letters about him are repetitious. But the reader will, I think, find both selections worth leafing through, at least.

S.A.

Before answering them specifically, I should tell you that I have the highest regard and affection for Nelson. . . . He is the same wonderful fellow to-day that he always has been, and we all love him.

As sophomores I was responsible for collecting the money for our fraternity picture. The price was fifty cents unframed and a dollar framed. When I told this to Nelson he said he would take it unframed for he could frame it for less than fifty cents.

When Nelson was here in Venezuela in November right after the elections, he reminded me that one of his first experiences in politics was when he and I ran against each other for the presidency of the senior class at Dartmouth. Nelson and I had moved in pretty much the same circles at Dartmouth and if either one of us had run alone, the one who did run would have won the election fairly easily. What actually happened was that we split the vote and a third (and very deserving) candidate stepped in and nosed us both out. This proves, I suppose, that neither he nor I was much of a politician back in those days.

Nelson was then, always has been, and still is a born leader. I am sure that Nelson's ability to make and keep friends, his intelligent, enthusiastic and all-out approach to any problem, his liberal philosophy which somehow has evolved out of a highly conservative heritage, and a whole lot of just plain executive ability would have meant that Nelson today would have been an important public figure even if his name had not been Rockefeller.

I not only was in college with Nelson; I worked for him and with him for twelve years after graduation and therefore feel that I know him well.

In case any of the above sounds as though I might be trying to gain a few points with the boss, I should point out that I haven't worked for Nelson since 1943.

While his name and fortune may have been a hurdle between him and easy companionship with the rest of his class and college mates, it was one which he had little difficulty clearing. He went a long way toward overcoming this hurdle during his first week at college. I know of no count that was made of the number of rugs he beat and rooms of furniture he moved for upper classmen during those first days, but it is certain that most of the latter preferred to have their work done by a Rockefeller, if available, than any one of the rest of us and he was unable to make himself very scarce. The good grace with which he took this indoctrination to undergraduate life gave him a fine start in his very successful undergraduate career. As you know, he went on to become a member of the varsity soccer team, a Senior Fellow and was president of both The Arts and The Dartmouth Pictorial, to which he was a liberal photographic contributor.

Always an extrovert and friendly, he had and apparently still has the personality for a natural politician and there is no question but what he has the mental ability, judgment and fortitude to make an outstanding statesman.

If Nelson had gone to Dartmouth under any other name, no one would have known him as anyone except a normal college student. He was as much a part of us as any other friend. Nelson won many honors, both scholastically and socially, but he won them on merit and would have won them no matter what his name. In my opinion he is one of the most self-effacing persons that I have ever known.

Personally, I would vote for him anytime but whether the average man will accept his personification of Capitalist remains to be seen.

"Rocky" had the ability to make others feel perfectly at ease. Sometimes boys who first met him might have been impressed because he was the grandson of "John D." but it was not long before everyone liked him for himself and never gave a thought to the significance of his name.

"Rocky" was a great credit to his heritage. He never imbibed as others did during prohibition; he never smoked, and certainly led a good Christian life.

I recall that during Fraternity days, on Wednesday meeting nights, it was a requirement that the boys wear detachable stiff collars. "Rocky" used to be kidded because he would wear a formal shirt, as he did not want to spend the money for a regular shirt. I also recall the time he was kidded by many about going home to New York with a large rip in his trousers. There was another story about the time his father and mother came to visit him, and they were entertained by President Hopkins. On leaving, President Hopkins' daughter, Ann, asked the Rockefellers to give her a lift up town. On the way, Mr. Rockefeller told his chauffeur to pull into the Standard station for gas, and immediately Ann told the chauffeur to go across the street to the Texaco station, as her father had often said that they sold better gasoline, so Mr. Rockefeller directed the chauffeur to go to the Texaco station. "Rocky" used to laugh and enjoy being kidded about such incidents.

In college, Nelson was a big, handsome lad with a friendly smile and an unassuming attitude. He was one of the most liked and respected boys in the class, and was on a first-name basis with all the boys. In those days, the conventional garb of the Dartmouth undergraduate was white duck pants and a dark green (Dartmouth green) crew-neck sweater. When the temperature went down—as it frequently did to below zero— we wore sheepskin-lined coats, knee length or shorter, and wool knit caps or "beanies" of the Dartmouth green. When the melting snows made the campus a sea of water and mud, we added galoshes, which were worn unbuttoned and flapping. Nelson dressed according to this custom, as did practically all of the 2,000 or so undergraduates.

One amusing incident he might recall was on a visit to West Point. The game was scheduled late in the afternoon, and toward the end of the game, the sun went down. This was signalled by firing a cannon, and all cadets came to attention to salute the stars and stripes as they were being lowered, including the cadets on the playing field. At that instant, the Dartmouth boys had the ball, and proceeded through the cadet line, which stood at attention like rigid mummies, and put the ball in the net for a goal before the referee awakened to the situation and called a time-out.

My first recollection of the name Nelson Rockefeller was after I'd been four weeks a Freshman. There weren't many job opportunities available for Freshmen who might want to help themselves financially through school. A fellow could, however, if he was lucky get a job waiting on table at one of the many private eating clubs in Hanover. As I recall it was about four weeks after school started that word got around that one of our classmates by the name of Nelson Rockefeller, who really was a son of John D. Jr., had gotten himself a job waiting on table at one of these clubs. The management, however, upon learning his identity persuaded him to give up the job in favor of someone else who might need the money more than he.

As fellow members of the Arts, a student organization which, among other things, entertained visiting celebrities, Nelson and I served as joint hosts to Edna St. Vincent Millay. Since Nelson was, and, as far as I know, still is a complete teetotaler, I carried the ball alone in providing liquid refreshments for Edna after she became bored with the reception we had arranged for her through the English Department and the Library. The following day Edna and her husband, who had accompanied her, and I were nursing hangovers, while Nelson was his usual fresh and energetic self.

There were many people in our Class who were closer to Nelson than I was, and who have seen more of him since graduation than I have, but to sum up my evaluation of Nelson it would appear to me that he is eminently well qualified, both by temperament as well as ability, to handle his assignment as Governor of New York, and to serve as President of the United States, if that should be his destiny.

In his whole college career, Nelson was "one of the boys." He has always had a genuine interest in and liking for people, no matter who they are or where they came from, and his friendships in the class were wide. Answering your specific questions, he was extremely well liked, and his wealth was no bar to easy companionship with the other students. He was an extrovert and gregarious. At the same time, he required occasional periods of solitude, especially before exams, when he would bury himself for days in some place like Woodstock. He maintained the highest standards of personal conduct (he didn't smoke, swear or drink) without any trace of a holier-than-thou attitude. His normal appearance —a crew cut, dirty corduroy pants and a green sweater—was as sloppy, if not more so, than the college average. He was exuberant, loved rough-housing and participated in such dubious ventures as the kidnapping of the leading members of one of the other classes.

In financial matters, there was no show of wealth, one reason being that he had no wealth to show. He was on a rather strict allowance and accounted regularly to his father. Although his expenditures were very moderate, there were a number of times when he was completely out of cash and was obliged to borrow from his roommate.

In his studies he was a hard, conscientious (though not a brilliant) worker with an inquiring mind which brought him into more after-class contacts with the professors than most people had. . . . His spelling was (and probably still is) atrocious, and he had to make a special deal with the English Department, which had a rule that any theme with more than a certain number of misspellings would automatically flunk.

This was the era of the Kellogg-Briand pact, which we thought had eliminated war forever; of the Hoover prosperity and the booming stock market. The 1929 crash made very little impression on us. We had no reason to question the status quo. I would think it fair to say that Nelson, along with the rest of us, accepted the existing order pretty much as it was.

There is one story that answers several of your questions. I labelled it "When I threw millions over my shoulder"—, never dreaming that today he would be Governor of New York, and with the possibility of being President.

It occurred one night in our senior year at the Casque and Gauntlet house. For some reason or other I was first in bed in our dormitory. I was almost asleep when a couple of room-mates crept in and turned over somebody's bed. I stayed awake to see who came next, and it was Nelson. I watched as he made his way down the room to go to bed and then, evidently thinking I was responsible for the sculduddery, came crawling up on his hands and knees to tip my bed over. As he jumped for mine, I was ready, and threw him over my shoulders. We both felt like wrecks for a while, but had a good laugh.

A small bit of college give-and-take roughhouse, perhaps, but it is an indication of the regular kind of guy he was, even then.

Nelson Rockefeller's father, John D. Rockefeller, Jr., spoke at a dinner during our graduation in 1930. If I remember correctly (1930 is so long ago) he told us to live so (that is, with such integrity) that we could tell anyone to go to hell at any time of our lives. I'm not sure that that is valid advice but I was impressed then and they are the only words I remember out of the entire graduation week.

His interest in teaching Sunday School in Vermont was due to his normal interest and respect for this activity and he did not do it to conform, please his parents or because it might have been expected of him. He was just thoroughly wholesome, in a very masculine way and was always on the "go."

In our days of Prohibition while at school it was "smart," of course, to have several drinks at any of the few social functions we had. Nelson neither drank nor smoked; however, he was not critical of those who did and was no prude on the subject. He would have such a good time at a house party dance and would be charging around the dance floor as enthusiastically as those who were slightly in their cups. . . . He had boundless energy and it was directed in the proper channels. He never paraded as a "Rockefeller" and he took pains to try to hide his identity, since he wanted to be accepted as a "regular guy."

Visiting with the Rockefellers for these three days was like dropping in on the Joneses. There was no sign of class distinction, ostentation, or privilege, and their welcome was warm and honest. They were totally disarming in manner and most of us had a charming vacation before settling down to whatever jobs we could find in 1930.

. . . he wore the same type corduroy knickers during the winter that everyone else wore, and they weren't any cleaner than the other fellow's after a long winter. He did not have an unusually large ward-robe and he was not a flashy dresser. He was not fastidious about keeping an orderly room, which was in keeping with his C & G brothers. He was alert to someone trying to shine up to him because he was a "Rockefeller," but he was kind in dealing with this type and did not hurt their feelings. He was tolerant in argument, but dogged in his devotion to a "cause."

Nelson's spelling was terrible. This deficiency was due, I believe, to his progressive secondary education at the Lincoln School. During English exams his professor would tell him to put a question mark after all words whose spelling he questioned. There were question marks all over his blue books. He

would ask us how to spell connected words such as whom-
ever, nevertheless, since he could not grasp these words from
his progressive schooling background.

In summary on Nelson: he was gregarious, friendly, unassuming, vigorously athletic, companionable, full of drive—
this composite spells out a natural, honest politician of the
Eisenhower type. His character, then and now (I had a conference with him less than a year ago), is one to invite respect
and honor. There is nothing cheap or superficial about him.
He is a "good guy."

I hope that I have given you some honest answers to your
inquiry.

In passing, I might say that I am the fellow who ran for
Junior Class President against Nelson and I had the tremendous good fortune to defeat him at that time. It seems to me
Dartmouth College deserves some credit for the breadth of
her education, when the son of a poor shoe worker could defeat the son of such a wealthy and famous family.

In the past this accomplishment meant a lot to me, but in
the light of Nelson's popularity and success in the State of
New York and his potentiality as a candidate for the Presidency of the United States, I am sure it is gathering importance in my own mind.

I hope you may find some small idea here that would help
you make American people and the people of the world realize how fortunate we are to have Nelson available.

At Dartmouth he was, if not the *worst* dressed boy in his
class, he came pretty close to being the most casually dressed.
He just didn't care about "show" and he did like to be comfortable. Dartmouth's a pretty democratic school, anyway,
and, really, the idea that he might have quite a bit of money
didn't seem to enter into his friendships and his acquaintances—here again, in a small school like Dartmouth he got to
know almost everyone in the class, as most of us did. He was,

indeed, very well liked by all of his classmates, *and still is!*

I remember him vividly at the time of the annual Fresh-man-Sophomore "rush," which always turned into a chaotic melee. There was so much shoving and pushing going on be-tween about 1,000 members of the Freshman and Sophomore classes that I saw him only briefly with his shirt torn off his back, laughing like crazy and having the time of his life.

He has a great joy for life, he is full of zest, and always was —in a way, I wouldn't be surprised if he has a lot of the same ebullience and energy and love of life that characterized Teddy Roosevelt.

There are many fine things I could say about Mr. Rocke-feller, but the thing that stands out in my mind above all else is a statement he made during a discussion we had during the latter part of our senior year. This was in the spring of 1930. The depression was upon us. In our group as we sat around one evening we reported on what we planned to do after graduation. Some were planning to go into business, some law, a few in medicine, and I was planning to become a teacher.

In somewhat of a joking way the question was put to Nel-son along these lines: "How in the world are you ever going to get a job and support yourself during this depression?" "What are you going to do?" After some informal joking about this he answered in all seriousness somewhat along these lines: "My job will be to take the wealth that will come under my direction and use it to do the greatest good for the greatest number of people."

Nixon: *Whittier High School*

I did not know "Dick" intimately—just well enough to say "hello" to him in the halls. However, I admired him *very* much, and was not a bit surprised that he attained renown, for he was such an outstanding person, intellectually and in character and personality. I can't imagine him being dishonest or unscrupulous as he has at times been labelled in past years. He exhibited a degree of egotism but it was not obnoxious, rather a justified faith in himself which no doubt enabled him to push ahead as he did.

In our Junior year we were in the same English class, I remember only one incident in that class that year that concerns Nixon. We were all to make a ten minute speech on the

Constitution. Our Teacher was a little white haired maiden
lady. The day we were to start making our Orations in class
she invited the head of the English Department, Miss Jennie
B. McGregor, in to hear the speeches. She started down the
line of seats, calling on four different students and no response. Then she came to Miss Ola Florence Welch (you have
written to her as Mrs. Gail Jobe), Ola Florence got up and
gave a pretty fair oration, at least she gave it word for word
as the written copy that she had handed to the teacher. How
many more were called on before she came to Richard I do
not remember, none responded. On Richard's turn he arose,
handed her the copy and began! That was the first oration I
had ever heard and probably the best, it was Richard's first.
He gave it before the class and Miss Jennie B. as though we
were Congress. It was great. The teacher was so mad because
so few had responded that she did not appreciate it though,
and kept making minor corrections as he deviated a word
from his written text. When he was through she called on
more and finally called on me. I got up, gave her my copy and
started. She made a minor correction and as I tried to go on
she made another and I ground to a halt and quit. She dismissed the Department Head and then did we catch it! She
was the most mortified that she had ever been, etc. etc. We
made such a miserable showing before the Head of the Department, etc. I have felt for years that she sure missed the
boat. Here she was listening to a speech, his first oration, of
a future President of the United States and she was so mad
at a bunch of kids that she didn't even hear it. I expect that
Richard felt as bad as the rest of us about the bawling out
we got, it didn't faze us a bit.

Sorry to be so long answering your request for information
on Richard Nixon. We wished to ask his permission before we
wrote to you.

Even in high school, Dick's classmates predicted that he

would be a future president of the United States. As a Junior at Whittier High, (Dick attended Fullerton High his first two years), he was noted for his oratory. He eliminated twelve other students and won first prize speaking on "Our privileges under the Constitution." In a district contest at that time, he won from South Pasadena High.

In 1930 he was the Student Body General Manager and president of the Scholarship Society. He was a member of the Latin Club and wrote features for the *Cardinal & White,* our weekly school paper. This year, also, he won first prize in the Oratorical Contest speaking on "American progress—its dependence on the Constitution." *The Los Angeles Times* presented him a prize for his essay. In the district contest he won second place. Both this speech and the one in his Junior year were printed in our school annual. We always enjoyed hearing him for his speeches were most entertaining. This year he spoke at the Junior-Senior banquet.

The class prophecy predicted "In the city of Los Angeles ——. Here, too, is Richard Nixon. He sponsors the *Times* Oratorical Contests which are still going strong."

In thinking back, I am reminded of high school days when he won the championship for the debating team of Whittier Union High School. He became pretty much of a hero in all our eyes for that put Whittier Union on the map for the first time. We couldn't help but recognize his outstanding ability as a public speaker, even then.

If the honor of becoming the President of the United States should come to Richard Nixon, I can think of no one better endowed for the tremendous task ahead.

As a scholar, he was easily at the head of the class. I feel sure that the high moral background given him by his mother and father will continue to keep him earnestly seeking to give the straightforward type of leadership that people can respect.

Nixon: Whittier College

 . . . I think this is important for it shows *what made Nixon great*. He was not an Athlete, neither was I, they did not have enough Freshmen out to make a legal Freshmen Football Squad, they needed one more, a substitute. I had just gotten a job as a Soda Jerk in a Drugstore and with a Chemistry Major I thought it very important so I refused to help them. They asked Dick and for the good of the School he went out, he did better than expected, much better. About this time they discovered he could talk. A football player who could talk—who could really make speeches, good speeches, interesting speeches. The College needed more High School graduates to come to Whittier, football players too. Whittier was one of the best small schools at football. He was in, he went around to all the High Schools making speeches on what it was like to play football at Whittier College. His "Speech" was a big success because, as always, he told the truth. He started out by saying, "you know the reason I play football for Whittier College, it is so I can make this speech." It just laid the kids in the aisle. Then he went on with a good pep talk for Whittier. He was not controversial at all, there were no arguments or incriminations about Dick. I think the controversy in late years has come from Jealousy and the fact that any exposer of corruption Dick made showed up some of his own party as well as the opposition. He is too good for them. Along side of him they look selfish. If Dick is a pusher it is because he is trying his best for his country. Somebody needs to do his best. And Dick is good, much better than we thought. He is the best. In fact I think he will be in. He sold Whittier College to the High School students, I think he can Sell our Ideals to the backward peoples. He has exposed spies and corruption in Government. Sure he may be a little rough. Remember his first important Presidential Election was the one Roosevelt defeated Hoover. Don't think that wasn't rough.

At Whittier College Dick and I were close. We double-dated a lot and we were both charter members of the Orthogonia Athletic Fraternity. Dick was taken into this organization to give the group some dignity, scholastically speaking. Our founders did not want us to be known as an unintelligent bunch of athletes. You see this relationship sort of forced Dick into going out for football.

Dick was not universally popular in college because he was not what you would call a real friendly guy and, as most scholars, he had little time for activities which resulted in popularity. Many students felt Dick was above them in thinking and that probably he didn't care to associate with them. Of course there was the usual discontent among the school's fraternities.

Dick lived somewhat abnormally. He studied a great deal
and worked in the store. It wasn't uncommon for him to work
himself ill. On one occasion Dick was home ill. His mother
called me at the college and asked to have his books brought
home. When I arrived Dick was really ill with the flu. His
home and rooms were moderate. Dick was worried about his
lessons and grades; he was extremely interested in how things
were going at school and the welfare of his friends.

When Dick became a senior in college he participated in
more social affairs—mainly dancing. He was a poor dancer
and not in demand, but a real gentleman.

The most outstanding accomplishment I recall about Dick
Nixon was his going out for Varsity football three years and
getting the "hell" knocked out of him, but staying with it and
lettering. I was captain of that college team and I think his
football training had a lot to do with the strengthening of
those important human attributes of learning to take it, stay
with it, and team play. I imagine he will always treasure the
friendship of his football teammates.

I wouldn't say that Dick was entirely popular but I would
say that he was greatly respected for the reasons which you
already know and those that I have attempted to state in this
letter.

Much of Dick's political career has been influenced by
fortuitous circumstances. Although Nixon no doubt would
have been a student leader at any school he might have attended, he moved almost automatically into such a position
at Whittier College. He had been the fair-haired boy at
Whittier Union High School, a large, high-rated high school,
not more than a half mile distant, which had always contributed far more heavily toward the college student body than
any other school. He had advanced far in the elimination trials
of a national interscholastic debating organization. He had

been *the*—or *a*—leader scholastically. He had been high school student body president.

Hence, on his arrival at college, along with reputation and a large band of constituents, he could hardly have become other than a student leader. During his four years, he seldom had serious competition for office of any organization appropriate to his class and his interests.

The principal factor in the personality of the Richard Nixon I remember seems to be an incredible combination of enthusiasm and energy.

As to enthusiasm, I used to wonder if it was wholly genuine and, if not, how much was real and how much was simulated for the benefit of all present. For instance, at a pregame rally, it is sometimes difficult to believe that the lamb can be incited to seriously resist the slaughter; or that the pitifully meager turn out could, by sheer noise, destroy the enemy. Nevertheless, Dick usually managed to put a little or a lot of fire into his audience. I believe that most of his enthusiasm was real.

As to energy, he sometimes seemed to be pushing himself along a course of thought or action, and tending to push others along at his pace. It was almost as if he had once upon a time taken a vow always to do his utmost. Although this feeling of pressure or urgency was actually only an impression in the mind of the one feeling pushed, it could be a little wearing merely because it seemed a little too hard for the slower-acting—and, possibly, the slower-thinking—remainder of us to keep up.

Whittier College is a small denominational institution and is—or, at least in those times, was—highly moral. In other words, there was probably far less smoking, drinking, premarital experimentations, and other assorted vices than would have been found in a typical high school. As always, however, there were many who thought, spoke, or acted with fewer inhibitions than others. I have always considered Dick to be a member of the very moral set. But between the moral and the slightly immoral there was, at least so far as Dick was concerned, no snooty barrier.

As a kindly, democratic, and somewhat "commonplace," yet very powerful leader or ruler, Dick had few, if any, serious rivals. During my four years at Whittier, I do not believe I heard a single derogatory remark about him. Neither do I recall anyone making a point of singing his praises. Possibly there were small anti-Nixon groups or individuals outside my circle of acquaintance. In general, it was just a matter of his being well liked and considered the best man for the job in question.

Consequently, I was rather surprised when Dick seemed to become even more of a whipping boy for the political opposition than other vice presidents.

My chief impression on looking back is that he was extremely intelligent and capable but—at least to me—a bit of a "stuffed shirt." Even then he was an excellent speaker and there was no doubt of his ability.

I do not ever remember hearing any mention of a lack of trustworthiness, as we sometimes do now. In fact I cannot conceive of anyone with his Quaker background being anything but honest.

Dick was always what I've termed, a "fireball": if he was sold on a matter, it was his nature to do something, come what might. He was willing to lead and eager to follow if someone else had taken the initiative.

In those trying times of the early thirties, gala social affairs were rare. However, in the fall of '33, I was invited to a formal girl date affair. I knew Dick had just splurged and bought a new tuxedo. I also knew he had an old one which someone had given him. I asked him to lend me his old tux and although he was going to the same affair, I almost had to fight him to keep him from outfitting me in his new tux!

The 1929 crash and ensuing depression raised havoc with
Whittier College's budget as it did with all private colleges.
As an economy measure, baseball was dropped as a college
sport in the spring of 1932. Being a baseball bug, I was trying
to revive the sport in 1933 by circulating a petition, for all
interested players to sign. Knowing Dick didn't even pretend
to be a baseball player, I hadn't thought of approaching him.
He hunted me up and insisted on signing my petition, maintaining that no college should be without baseball!

If I sound biased in my thinking, it is because I am! By
and large, I have an abiding faith in the integrity of American statesmen and politicians. But I *know* Dick Nixon! You
can't spend four years on the same football squad with a man
and not come to know what makes him tick. Truly, here is a
realistic, practical man with a brilliant mind and an undying
interest in his fellow man! Here, I *know*, is a man who measures up to the biggest job in the world, in *all* respects!

. . . on a campus of only about 400 students it goes without saying that I did gain impressions of Richard Nixon as a
student leader. One of them is that there was always about
him an intensity of purpose, a tremendous drive which was
perhaps in itself what made him seem brusque, almost brash.
He was not generally liked by the girls whom I knew best,
one of whom detested his admitted cockiness.

In regard to this trait, let me state that, in my own opinion,
without this cocksure streak in his nature, it would scarcely
have been possible for him, an obscure young man, to have
risen so fast in the political world.

One remark my husband made in his recollection of Dick
was that he seemed to show very little sense of humor at that
time.

A friend, also of the class of '34, with whom I have talked
since receiving your letter recalls a college gathering in our
student days, probably a student assembly, at which Dick

Nixon stated that he wanted to go into politics and that he felt the field was dominated by too many unscrupulous politicians.

I'm sure you've heard about the number of hours Dick spent at his Dad's store and gas station in East Whittier. How he managed to get top grades, be a student leader, take part in dramatics, debate, four years of football, start a flourishing new men's society and have time to be a friendly, popular guy, I'll never know. Most of us had a tough time maintaining a "C" average and not doing a tenth of the other things that Dick did.

I don't remember that he had too much time for dates or casual campus horseplay. I'm sure the reason was that there weren't enough hours in the day for the non-essentials. Still I'm sure nobody thought of Dick as a stuffed shirt—even the Franklins. Everyone admired his determination to play football and his real ability in every other thing he undertook.

Without too much conversation about it, I know we all had the feeling that Dick's leadership, his sincerity and ability would someday make him a real leader and I know too, that without exception, we were all pulling for him.

It is not often one has the opportunity to know a political leader personally. May I say that having done so, it is with the greatest faith that I unhesitatingly endorse him for I sincerely believe he feels dedicated to the service of his country. I know his intensity for those principles in which he believes. His ability is unquestionable. Knowing his family background and the atmosphere of his formative years, he is truly the epitome of what one should like to use as an example of a typical American middle-class boy risen by the token of his personal efforts and abilities.

Dick was not a social butterfly but he did attend the functions. The college gave its first sanction to a dance when we were Freshmen, and Dick's main promise when a Junior was a dance a month if elected President of the student body. This action coming from a Quaker, I think, showed progressive thinking. You will recall that in those days no church sanctioned dancing, but today many include it in their social activities. This one instance showed Dick was wise enough to see what the students wanted and that dancing under proper sponsorship was better than having them go elsewhere for their social life. There were other progressive ideas put forth by Dick with reference to other activities of the student body, but I mention this particular instance to show that Dick was not one who is narrow minded in his thinking.

I think Dick was universally popular as he was friendly to all and very seldom did you hear an unkind word about a fellow student, but see some underhanded act on the field of athletics and no one could yell louder than Dick. Dick always liked a good clean battle, either on the field of athletics or in the debating room, and he has probably made enemies because of his hard hitting tactics, but I believe you will find he fights fair as he did in those days. From my association with Dick and the way he felt about his fellow students, I feel he will always try to give the people what they want and need, if within reason and at all possible.

In those days at Whittier, there was one boys' dormitory. These fellows played pranks which make pretty good stories. I can't remember Nixon as ever being involved in any of these, I may be wrong. As a matter of fact I would be surprised if he had been.

On the other hand, he was into everything. He was on every team or project, and not because he was particularly good at everything either. It didn't seem to make much difference to him. He liked to participate and be part of a team.

He was a student professors love—earnest and eager to learn. I believe in the classes we had together, which were not too many, he was considered one of the "average raisers," if you know what I mean. Some of the kids wrote answers on their cuffs. I believe I'd say Nixon did it the hard way.

He was the type of fellow who would be on time even if the boss was on vacation, and you know how unpopular this makes a person with the others.

As I recall he wasn't afraid to tell what he believed. In 1934, things looked pretty bleak. An A.B. entitled you to work on the W.P.A. It was easy to turn against everything which had been to something new. My recollection of Nixon was that he was sticking to what he believed regardless of anything.

In 1954, twenty years after our graduation, our class had a special reunion at Whittier. I hadn't been back since graduating. Nixon at this time was Vice President and of course I was flattered to be included in this group. I did not believe that he would remember me as the "one who used to read poetry." Then and now, I really don't care how he did it; maybe a secretary looked it up for him; maybe he sat up all night learning something about everybody who would be there. As I say it really doesn't matter how he did it, it was special and I liked it.

There were others at school, boys on the teams, who knew Nixon much better. Today they are apt to recall that Nixon had to learn how to have fun and he did.

No student who was in many of the same classrooms with Dick as I was could fail to detect a brilliant student. His high scholarship ratings put him in a class by himself. So much higher, in my particular case, that I became one of hundreds who secretly admired and envied him more than he realized. His keen intellect and powers of concentration made it possible for him to stand head and shoulders above his classmates, approaching at times the realm of a genius. Dick was always intensely earnest in every assignment and astounded me with the vast amount of knowledge immediately forthcoming on any subject.

One incident stands out in my mind so vividly that I shall never forget it. One warm Spring afternoon in 1933 in a psychology class, Professor Newlin, a senior member of the faculty in his 70's, expounded his theories on the workings of the subconscious mind as related to our reasoning faculties. Dick challenged his synopsis, and in a 45-minute discussion along with Professor Newlin (the rest of us were lost in the fine technicalities of its depth) brought about an admission by this esteemed authority in his field that Mr. Nixon had completely changed his thinking which he had been expounding over the lecture stand for years. After the class was dismissed many of us congratulated him and I slapped him on the back, making this comment: "Dick, if you ever get into politics you'll never stop until you're President of the United States." He very shyly shrugged his shoulders and passed it off with a laugh.

His perception of weaknesses in an opponent's statements were unmistakably demonstrated in his debating abilities. On the Whittier College debating team he was invincible, and certainly opposing team members realized this most. Never argumentative, but always constructive in his remarks, he would sway opinion in his direction in a very few minutes, almost always without notes and without exception in most demonstrative physical gestures—"straight from the shoulder" with set jaw and a decisive glint in his eye. He is a natural-born orator in my humble opinion.

Dick was always a very serious student, not easily invoked to laughter or frivolity. He was always neat and punctual in every detail and built up a tremendous popularity in student government affairs with determination and a driving force to see the best aims of the College realized. I never felt that his seriousness was a handicap, but I did have a feeling that a slight sense of jealousy was engendered by his rivals, merely on the basis that Dick was very seldom unable to channel his ideas in such a way to meet and defeat every objection.

His overwhelming personality cannot be explained. He is as common as the proverbial "old shoe." He is always the same, a fact proven in my mind when our class of '34 met him in person 20 years later in Whittier just before he delivered the commencement address to the class of 1954 as Vice-President of the United States. My wife said: "Isn't he an interesting person—so friendly and genuine." She had never met him before.

Dick sensed his "unpopularity" among his friends who thought he was not entirely a "regular guy" by going out for football in his Senior year. Although he rode the bench most of the season, coach Chief Newman was very proud of his name on the team roster and I shall never forget the tremendous roar which went up from the rooting section when Dick got into the line-up for the last few minutes of a few games. One had to admire his gameness, for he was trying to overcome a psychological factor which he and all of us knew—he just wasn't meant to be a football player. But he tried and it made him unanimously popular on and off the campus.

As a member of a conservative Quaker family, he made it a point to respect the fundamentals he had been obviously taught. While he attended most of the college social functions, his behaviour was always in the best of taste, and I never saw him in any other light than a perfect gentleman. He was popular with the girls, but never seemed over-interested to my knowledge. I never saw him smoke or drink, nor did I hear profanity or obscene language from his lips. I am certain he is a perfect husband and a devoted father.

Only in one college course did I feel near an equal with Dick. In Shakespeare we were both pretty sad, although he got a "B" and I got a "C." I still think I deserved a "B" with him. Maybe it was because he was a drama student and took

leading roles in several school plays, among which he must
have used some Shakespeare.

In summary let me say that I would not hesitate to recom-
mend him and wish for him all the honors our country can
bestow upon him—including the Presidency which I may
have predicted years ago. Knowing the background of this dy-
namic personality, as I had the pleasure of developing
through my school days, I am sure he has all the qualities
necessary to make him invincible in world leadership among
the world's greatest minds—even greater minds than Alger
Hiss once thought he had. "He's our boy" and we would like
to be able to some day say "we told you so."

Nixon: Duke University Law School

. . . I shall endeavor below to summarize my recollections of Dick Nixon as a law student as objectively as possible. I say this because, as something of a civil libertarian, I have in past years been deeply disturbed over Nixon's apparent unconcern with the heavy attacks leveled against constitutional liberties by McCarthy and others—and with his own participation in such attacks from time to time. Consequently, I shall, as nearly as I can, make no observations as of 1937.

Dick Nixon was liked and respected by all of the members of the Class of '37. He was our class president during the senior year. But I do not believe he had many close personal friends among his classmates. He was popular in the class, but

I would describe it as a sort of "lonesome" kind of popularity.

Nixon was not only considered a particularly hard worker, he was a prodigiously hard worker, and was highly respected for it.

As to political views during law school, rightly or wrongly, and until the election of 1946, I had always regarded Dick Nixon as a New Deal supporter.

As a matter of negative recollection, I cannot recall during law school days at any time hearing Nixon make a remark that would indicate any kind of racial or religious bias on his part. I believe that in common with the balance of his classmates from the North and West he was shocked and disturbed at the prevalent North Carolina treatment of the negro population as an inferior group.

. . . Nixon is the ablest man I have ever known in public life, and one of the too small number of public men in whom I would have genuine confidence to handle a problem of mine if he were to step into private life.

Now for your specific inquiries.

Nixon had many friends at Duke. With the usual reservation about absolutes, I should say that Nixon was liked by everyone. . . . The liking for Nixon was not so extreme as to make him a glamour boy, but was almost universal in the normal way. He was considered a regular guy, who liked people and who was liked in return. He tended somewhat towards shyness, but the small size of the school and the resulting friendly nature of the student body got past any barriers of shyness which might have restricted his circle of friends in a larger institution.

He was a very hard worker. He nearly, if not completely, worked his way through school and still managed to be third in a class of very intelligent, eager, hardworking students. One member of the class insists that to this day he has never seen anyone who worked as hard as Nixon did in law school.

Our last year in law school four of us, including Nixon and myself, lived in a small place out in the Duke forest about a mile from the law school which was nicknamed "Whippoor-will Manor." The place had no utilities or conveniences of any kind, and it wasn't very sturdily constructed. In the winter-time it could get pretty damp and chill in the one room where the four of us slept in two double beds. There was some heat which could be supplied by stuffing tightly balled up paper into a small sheetmetal laundry stove which would heat up very fast when the paper was lighted. However, it wasn't feasible to light another paper fire for some little time after one had been set, so that when we stuffed the stove with paper at night before we went to bed it was understood there could only be one fire in the morning. Nixon usually got up one or two hours before the rest of us, anywhere from 5:00 to 6:00 o'clock. We outvoted him on the matter of the stove, so that he couldn't light the fire, which meant that he got up in the chill and damp of the dawn, dressed in the dark or semi-dark without the benefit of any heat, and left for school in order to get in an hour or two of study before school started. This regime was necessitated by the library job he had, which I shall mention later. There were times when he luxuriated in bed so as to get up at 7:00 or shortly after with the rest of us, but not very often. I mention this to show that he not only worked hard, but he followed his schedule of hard work consistently in the face of rather strong temptations to take it easier.

There was nothing in the law school which could really be called politics. Once a year there was an election of the officers of the Student Bar Association, but that is all. The Spring of our second year Leon Rice, one of the top men of the Class of 1936, asked Dick to run for the presidency of the Student Bar Association for the year following, our Senior Year. I have seen this mentioned before as Nixon's first experience in politics, and I suppose you could call it that, but there was no

campaign or real preparation for the election. Nixon ran
against another member of our class, Hale McGown, now an
outstanding lawyer in Nebraska. McGown was very popular
and was engaged to one of the girls in our Class who was also
very popular. Nixon was elected. It was not my judgment that
the student body liked him better. I think probably the entire
student body of something over one hundred men and women
liked both Nixon and McGown, but the students were very
serious about the profession they were preparing for, and my
guess is that the factor which swung the election to Nixon
was genuine respect for his scholarship. On the other hand, I
think it is also clear that Nixon would not have been elected
on scholarship alone if he had not been personally liked.

There was nothing about Nixon or his interests then which
suggested to me or, as far as I know, to the others that he
would later follow politics as a career. My own guess is that
if politics had not sought out Nixon when that Citizens Committee was looking for a candidate to oppose Voorhis, Nixon
would never have sought out politics.

Nixon lived frugally, as did most of us. I have mentioned
our senior year at Whippoorwill Manor. This was a small
wooden house out in Duke forest which was rented by a Mrs.
Henderson and her son. As I recall, she was a widow and in
very straightened circumstances. We rented from her one
room large enough to contain two double beds and the stove
for $25.00 a semester, $50.00 a year. That made the total rent
for each of the four of us $12.50 for the year. All four of us
went down to the gym every day for some sort of exercise
and shower, except of course on Sunday. We kept clothes,
toilet articles, etc., stashed at various places around the school.
We tried to get to school enough in advance of classes each
morning to wash, shave, etc., and then go over to the Union for
a quick breakfast. The presidency of the Student Bar Association became really convenient for Nixon, because it gave
him an office in which to keep his clothes, toilet articles, etc.

Our second year in school I had an old 1926 seven (or nine) passenger Packard which I had saved from the junk yard for $40.00. We nicknamed the car "Corpus Juris." Nixon was one of those who rode around in it regularly. Every day nine of us went to lunch at a boarding house run by a Mrs. Pierce, where she served all a person could eat for 25 cents.

The spirit which prevailed in Corpus Juris during the ride out and back was a good deal like that in a locker room, friendly and boisterous. Every time we collected in the car the group climbed on someone's back and didn't let up until we reached the boarding house. Sometimes it was Nixon, sometimes it was someone else. In any event, Nixon was thoroughly at home in the horseplay and joined in both as subject and tormentor just like anyone else. This is not unusual, and I cite it only because I have read suggestions here and there to the effect that Nixon is a superficial, cardboard, calculating character who is not a regular fellow and who would not be at home in such circumstances. I assure you, this is not a true gauge of his personality.

Almost everyone in the class received a nickname at one time or another. There was Bull of the Woods, Senator (ironically, the Senator was Basil Whitener who is now a Representative from North Carolina), Boots Leathers, Pooh-pooh Perdue, etc. Nixon was of course called Dick or Nix, but in addition he acquired the nickname of Gloomy Gus. As I recall, this nickname came from a cartoon character who was always throwing the cold light of day on someone's rosy dreams, making comical situations. However, since the Gloomy part did not really fit, the nickname soon shortened down to just "Gus."

Nixon has always had a quiet but very definite sense of humor. . . . His humor was not slapstick, but subtle and very funny. I remember specifically that he delivered such an oration at the Senior Beer Bust, completely deadpan, but although I have now forgotten what he said either his speech was very funny or the beer was very effective, because he had everyone in the proverbial stitches.

I have been asked many times whether Nixon is a progressive, liberal, etc. One trouble about this is that here words have lost so much of their meaning. In my own book Nixon is a "true liberal." Among other things that means he believes individuals have responsibilities as well as rights. This was evident in law school in what many people could call a conservative approach, but one which was marked by a very powerful concern over the individual. He was a great admirer of Brandeis, Cardozo and Stone. I recall specifically that he felt very strongly the opposition of leading bar association officials to the confirmation of Brandeis to the Supreme Court was unjust and a mistake. On the other hand, in school he always exhibited antipathy toward philosophies which appeared to deprive an individual of responsibilities, which would be assumed for him by the social order. This, perhaps, was traceable to his Quaker background.

My impression was that Richard Nixon was not an exceptionally brilliant student, however, he was outstanding because of his ability to do prodigious amounts of work. He pursued his ambition to stand at the head of his class with an intensity that few people are capable of. I had the impression of Richard, at that time, that his only ambition and only desire was to master the subjects which he was taking in the law school and he did this with such an intensity of purpose that he spent every waking moment of his time in study.

I do not think that he was popular in the class. He had a few close friends and he stood very high in the esteem of the faculty, but at that time that he was a student in college, Richard Nixon was a person of very strong opinions. He had very strong moral convictions and he never let many opportunities go by to express himself on those convictions with a great deal of feeling and finality.

For instance, when I attended the Duke Law School I did so as a native of Tennessee. Richard had a very strong feeling in regard to the manner in which the negroes of the south had been mistreated. He looked upon the issue of the treatment of the negro in the south as a moral issue and condemned it very strongly as such, but did not realize the problems that confronted the people of the south in regard to the negro.

In college, Richard was a man of high moral standards and I was shocked to learn of his connection with those men and persons who were accused of contributing to his personal fortune in order to obtain political favors. I just never could believe that about Richard Nixon, having known him for three years while we were in the Law School together.

It is possible for me to believe that the accusations, made against him as a campaigner in which he indulged in some very questionable ethical tactics as far as pursuing his ambition to be elected to office was concerned, were true. He was a man of such high ambition and a man capable of pursuing his ambition with such intensity that I could more easily believe that he would and could do whatever was necessary to attain the goal that he had set for himself. However, I have serious doubts whether he himself did those things because I got the impression of Richard, in college, that he had very high morals and was motivated largely by a very high sense of duty.

You asked how did he live. Of course, at the time that we were in law school together, it was during the depression. Mr. Nixon attended the Duke Law School on a scholarship from Whittier, California. I got the impression that he was extremely poor. He worked in the library of the law school some and I never did see him spend any money that was not absolutely necessary. He was very frugal. In fact, I sort of got the impression that possibly he did not eat as regularly as most of us think a person has to in order to keep alive. I don't think he ate over two meals a day while I knew him in the law school. Eating seemed relatively unimportant to him.

You asked did he go to parties, if he did, I never heard of it. I never heard of him having a date with a girl the whole time he was in law school. Occasionally, I would see him at the gymnasium taking a little exercise. Most of the time that you saw Richard Nixon, while he was in law school, he was working. In my opinion, he was a very outstanding man, and of course, a man who pursued his ambition to master the subjects which he was studying in the school with the intensity that Richard Nixon did, is a person of high moral conviction, who had the courage to express himself intensely and with feeling, is not calculated to be popular with the students in a college atmosphere.

Of all of the students in the Duke Law School in the class of 1937, I would put him down as the man least likely to succeed in politics. We think of a politician as being a person of flexible standards, a man of compromise, a man who can weld together in a feeling of unity people of different viewpoints. Nixon did not have this quality at all. He was unbending and unyielding in his opinions and moral convictions, and incidently, was a very effective debater on such subjects. His life in the Duke Law School was the antipathy of all those things which we have come to think of as making a politician.

Before I make any comments about Dick Nixon I would like to tell you about my political affiliations, so you may discount the comments I make in any manner you see fit. I am a life-long Democrat—coming to voting age in 1931, when economic conditions were more rugged than they have ever been since.

May I start my comments on Dick Nixon by telling you of a conversation I had with an active life-long Republican in the Olympic Club of San Francisco when I was out there on business in the middle of December? This new acquaintance, when he found I had been in law school with Dick Nixon, asked me what he was like; I remarked that I never felt that I knew him very well—he replied, "No one in California knows Dick Nixon, either."

Everything Dick has been in national politics has borne out my original impression of him in law school—basically aloof, very sure of himself, and very careful to keep people from getting too close to him. As a politician he has had to create himself, because it has never been apparent what he really was from his actions. Without the hysteria of the McCarthy days I don't think he ever would have been noticed, yet he was smart enough to see what it would do for Dick Nixon. The philosophy he embraced drove the Dr. Condons and the Dr. Oppenheimers out of government, but today we're supposed to forget that phase of his life.

. . . I was a classmate of Mr. Nixon's at Duke University for only one year and that was a mighty long time ago.

However, I do remember him quite distinctly although I can't say I ever had a detailed conversation with him. He did not encourage comradeship.

My impression is that he was a very studious individual— almost fearfully so. I can see him sitting in the law library hunched over a book, seldom even looking up. He never smiled to my knowledge and wore a very solemn expression. You may have noticed his peculiar jaw construction. Well, in those days, it was even more pronounced and gave the man an unpleasing mien.

I believe Mr. Nixon had a financial struggle—as did many of the rest of us. I remember that he wore a reddish-purple sweater day after day, which is certainly not to his discredit. However, the image I have of Mr. Nixon is the sweater.

He may have been brilliant in school—I read in some article that he was—but he does not stand out in my mind as a superior student or individual during that first year of law school. Other members of the class do. Mr. Nixon's utter lack of personality may have dimmed his brilliance and his scholastic record would speak for itself.

As I remember Dick in Law School, he was certainly the antithesis of the Dick Nixon of today. In my opinion, he was the last person in the class one would have picked to become a political headline. Dick was serious, quiet, lived off the campus, kept pretty well to himself, and was definitely a hard worker. As I recall, he played a good game of table tennis.

In a small law school, as Duke was in those days, politics and parties played no part at all in our graduate school life. Like most of us, Dick also had an N.Y.A. job to keep the depression wolf from the door. As the record shows, he was an excellent student and finished near the top of the class.

. . . my contacts with him were mostly just at the law school as he was not the type of person to spend any time socializing, dating, but he was generally regarded by everyone as a student who was devoted to his work, and actually I think most of his classmates felt that Dick would very likely end up by being a law professor rather than landing right in the middle of politics. I am sure that there was no more studious or a more serious student at Duke during the whole time I was there than Nixon. On Saturdays when we went to football games or on Saturday nights and Sundays when most of the law students were doing a little celebrating or out courting some of the girls, Dick was usually in the library studying. He certainly gave no indication of being interested in women or in wasting his time socializing. The only time that I ever remember seeing him actually "let down his hair" and celebrate a little was a beer party which we had on an open lot near the school after graduation where we got a keg of beer and some softball equipment and went out and drank beer and had a softball game. I still remember seeing him try to catch a flyball out on the field with a glass of beer in

his hand. Although I was not as closely associated with him
as others, this is the only time that I ever recall his being out
with the boys and having something to drink.

I considered Dick Nixon at school, not only as a studious
sort of person and one dedicated to his studies, but I had the
impression that he was personally somewhat shy and he was
not one to engage in a lot of idle conversation but you usually saw him going around the school and speaking when he
was spoken to but in general devoting his entire time to his
studies.

It has been quite a long time and a lot has happened since
1936 and 1937, but I am sure you have found with your inquiry with the other members of this class that there was no
one who was more conscientious and I do not believe anyone
who was more honest and more forthright than was Nixon.
I have indicated above that I felt he was somewhat shy, he
was what I would term a modest individual and I still believe
today that regardless of the capacity in which he may serve
his country that there is not a more honest or more dedicated
individual in public life today.

Dick Nixon, very early in law school, impressed his classmates with his integrity and sincerity. He was in school on a
scholarship and also worked during his years at Duke, part of
the work being in the law library. As I recall, he also worked
in the law library two summers.

Dick was among the top three in his graduating class at 21.
Incidentally, the top man in our class made the highest three
year average of any student the law school has graduated.
Dick was a diligent and hard worker and his views in class
discussion and "bull sessions" were listened to with great respect. He had a faculty of quickly seeing the key issues in
any situation and always seemed to come up with a very
rational and reasonable solution.

I remember him most for his friendliness and sincere interest in the welfare of others. Although definitely not an extrovert, he still made friends easily and kept those friends.

. . . he was a very serious student and apparently had very little money. He did not mix particularly. My impression was he had the makings of a very good lawyer and I have never ceased to wonder why he went into politics.